York Press
322 Old Brompton Road, London SW5 9JH

Pearson Education Limited
Edinburgh Gate, Harlow, Essex CM20 2JE, United Kingdom
Associated companies, branches and representatives throughout
the world

© Librairie du Liban *Publishers* and Pearson Education Limited 2000

Stills and Screenplay © Canal+ Image International

First published 2000

ISBN 0-582-43182-4

Designed by Vicki Pacey
Phototypeset by Gem Graphics, Trenance, Mawgan Porth, Cornwall
Colour reproduction and film output by Spectrum Colour
Printed in Malaysia, KVP

# contents

**author of this note** Amanda Sheahan Wells has a BA Hons in Film Studies & Drama from the University of Kent and an MA in Film & Television Studies from Westminster University. She taught film studies to A Level and undergraduate students at South East Essex College for seven years. She now works as a journalist.

# background

# trailer

*A bout de souffle* seems to me the most original, insolently gifted and shattering work the young French directors have yet produced. Set down, the plot goes misleadingly like a routine thriller ... The treatment, however, is far from routine. Jean-Luc Godard makes a film as though no one had ever made one before.

*Penelope Gilliatt, The Observer, 9 July 1961*

far and away the most brilliant, most intelligent, and most exciting movie I have encountered this season.

*Roger Angell, New Yorker, 11 February 1961*

For once a cinema's advertisement does not exaggerate. The Academy advertises Jean-Luc Godard's *A bout de souffle* as 'the most eagerly awaited new film of the nouvelle vague', and certainly the film that *Sight and Sound* called 'the group's intellectual manifesto' is one that anyone with an interest in what the cinema is up to has been waiting to see.

*Isabel Quigly, The Guardian, 8 July 1961*

one might expect that a piece of film-making that was so radical and influential in its day would have suffered the traditional fate of seeming to have been overtaken by the developments set in train by its own success. Not so, however. With its mixture of fragmentation and intimacy, *A bout de souffle* still communicates a bracing shock of the new.

*Tim Pulleine, The Guardian, 21 July 1988*

the end of the old Cinema

'Anything goes' was the spirit behind *A bout de souffle*, and its portrayal of two characters lost in the labyrinths of existentialism burst like a thunderbolt on a world on the brink of social upheaval, making its director a god among youth and the movie the greatest cinematic achievement of the New Wave.

*1998 contempt.productions, http://contempt.net*

# reading a bout de souffle

*A bout de souffle*, also known as *Breathless* – its American release title – occupies a central place in film history and film study. Made in 1959, it provided a new approach to film production and film style, while its images and sounds captured the spirit of the post-war generation.

In an interview in *Films & Filming* in September 1961, Jean-Luc Godard said: 'I consider my *A bout de souffle* as being at the end of the old Cinema, destroying all the old principles rather than creating something new.' *A bout de souffle* can certainly be seen as a bridge between the films of the first half of the twentieth century and those of the second half. The film paid homage to the genres, stars and studios of the 'golden age of Hollywood' while also doing something new. It broke with the traditions of studio film-making and played with the conventions of film storytelling that Hollywood had made so successful. In an interview translated in Tom Milne's *Godard on Godard*, Jean-Luc Godard said: 'What I wanted was to take a conventional story and remake, but differently, everything the cinema had done' (p. 173).

*A bout de souffle* was both a critical and commercial success on its release. It won the Prix Jean Vigo in 1960, and the prize for best direction at the 1960 Berlin Film Festival.

The reputation of the film has lived on. It was re-released at the cinema in the UK in 1988 and on video in 1993.

Jean-Luc Godard's influence on some of the most dynamic modern film-makers is evident. Writing in *Village Voice* on 11 May 1972 Oliver Stone

A BOUT DE SOUFFLE

declared how, in his youth, he had 'fallen in love' with *A bout de souffle* and its central character. Jean-Luc Godard worked for a short time with Francis Ford Coppola at his Zoetrope studio in the early 1980s. Martin Scorsese, who re-released Jean-Luc Godard's 1963 film *Le Mépris* (Contempt) under his 'Martin Scorsese presents' banner, paid direct homage to *Le Mépris* in the music score of *Casino*. Quentin Tarantino drew inspiration from Jean-Luc Godard's 1964 film *Bande à part* (Band of Outsiders) for the dance competition scene in *Pulp Fiction*, and named his production company A Band Apart. However, Jean-Luc Godard's influence on modern film-making is not necessarily a stylistic one. What he, and the other young film-makers he was working with in France in 1959, did was to question, through critical analysis and film-making, the essence of what it was to be a film-maker.

# traditional hollywood cinema

To understand the impact of *A bout de souffle* it is necessary to look back to the way in which film-making had been organised and understood before 1959. The dominant mode of film-making was based in the Hollywood studio system. Film-making was centred around key studios such as Warner Brothers, Paramount and MGM. The studios employed all staff on contracts and allocated them to the production of films. Everyone involved in production, from the stars, directors and writers through to the designers, technicians and editors had limited choice over which films they worked on.

Hollywood at this time, between the 1920s and the 1950s, was organised around an industrial system of vertical integration, which meant that each studio had control over all aspects of its films. Each studio owned the production studios where their films were made, had all production staff on contracts, distributed and publicised the films themselves and then showed the films in their own cinemas. The profits for each film could then be ploughed back into the production of the next set of films.

# hollywood cinema background

Hollywood was organised ... for maximum efficiency

The studio system has often been referred to as a 'factory', albeit a 'dream factory'. This was partly because of the industrial ownership and control of the studios, but it also described the way in which films were produced. Films were being made for a mass, popular market, just as cars were at this time, and the production methods were not dissimilar. Specialised staff concentrated on just one aspect of a film's production, for example the design of the set or the writing of dialogue, just as a factory worker might concentrate on fitting one part of a car on an industrial production line. Hollywood was organised in this way for maximum efficiency. As soon as staff finished shooting one film the sets were changed and work started on the next film.

To support this efficient method of production a system of film storytelling, often referred to as the Classical Hollywood Narrative cinema, evolved as a sort of unwritten constitution. Everything, from camera set-up to the use of sound and editing followed a pattern. The pattern for film-making – the conventions of film-making – evolved gradually between the birth of cinema in 1895 and the mid 1930s, when sound cinema was fully established. Young film-makers learned their trade by working in junior positions on films. Everyone under-stood the conventions, and this made film-making a fast and efficient process.

# cahiers du cinéma & politique des auteurs

The industrial system of Hollywood production was considered by most as incompatible with the conventional view of 'art'. The traditional view of artists such as painters, novelists and musicians was that they worked alone, usually without concern for profit, as they pursued the genius of their work. The cinema, which involved lots of people in making a film for a mass audience in order to gain maximum profit, was assigned the status of 'mass entertainment' or 'low culture', in contrast to the serious 'high' arts of poetry and painting. It was certainly not considered worthy of serious critical attention.

However, things started to change, in France, in the period after the Second World War. The screening of all Hollywood films had been banned in France during Nazi occupation. Therefore, in the early post-war years, many of the Hollywood films produced between 1940 and 1945 were screened in quick succession, particularly in the Parisian cinéclubs.

The Cinémathèque Française in Paris, under the directorship of Henri Langlois, screened a wide variety of films, which gave its audience a thorough grounding in film history. Jean-Luc Godard was a regular visitor to the Cinémathèque, and it was here, during the late 1940s that he met and became part of a group of young intellectuals passionate about the cinema. This group included André Bazin, François Truffaut, Claude Chabrol, Jacques Rivette and Eric Rohmer: names that became synonymous with the theoretical writings of *Cahiers du cinéma*, and the film-making of the French New Wave.

*Cahiers du cinéma* revolutionised the critical appraisal of Hollywood cinema. The young writers, under the guidance of André Bazin, wrote critically about Hollywood genres of cinema such as the western and the gangster movie as no one had done before. The *Cahiers* writers theoretically analysed the form of films which had only ever been considered as commercial, popular entertainment.

More controversial was the *politique des auteurs*, a critical theory founded in *Cahiers du cinéma*, which called for a reconsideration of the role of the film 'creator' or auteur. The *Cahiers* critics studied the films of Hollywood directors such as Alfred Hitchcock, Howard Hawks and John Ford, and declared that these film-makers were auteurs, displaying a consistency in the style and themes of their work.

The *politique des auteurs* was the rallying manifesto of the young film critics, who wanted to challenge what they saw as the unimaginative approach to film-making in their native France. The *Cahiers* critics attacked the French cinema of 'quality' that existed at the time (mainly consisting of literary adaptations, in the same vein as modern films such as *Howards End* and *Sense and Sensibility*). Addressing twenty-one major directors of the day Jean-Luc Godard reportedly told them: 'Your camera movements are ugly because your subjects are bad, your casts act badly because your

# politique des auteurs background

dialogue is worthless; in a word, you don't know how to create cinema because you no longer even know what it is!'

# the french new wave

It was against this background that a new wave of film-making emerged in France. The term 'New Wave' (*Nouvelle Vague* in French) was coined by journalist Françoise Giroud at *L'Express* and referred to the group of films produced in France by new directors in 1959 and 1960.

The New Wave was the product of a number of circumstances combined. Firstly, the critical ideas and passion for the cinema of the young *Cahiers* critics transferred to film production as François Truffaut, Claude Chabrol, Jacques Rivette and Jean-Luc Godard made their first films during 1959. However, the impact of their films on the French and international market was helped by the wider circumstances of the time. General de Gaulle's Fifth Republic came to power in 1958, with the aim of modernising France by reforming French politics, economics and culture. The de Gaulle government, which wanted to showcase French culture, supported the films of the New Wave. At the same time the new medium of television was starting to affect film audiences, as people began to visit the cinema less regularly, and so French distributors were interested in backing films made by new directors for less money (see Contexts).

Developments in film technology also had a significant impact on the way New Wave films were made, and on the way they looked (see Style). New lightweight cameras, portable synchronous sound recorders and 'faster', more light-sensitive film stock meant that films could be made on location. As a result, film studios were not needed, crews could be smaller and therefore the films could be made more cheaply. Filming on location with hand-held cameras also meant that the new film-makers could experiment with the style of camera angles and camera movement, and the recording of sound. The changes in the conditions and methods of production employed by the New Wave film-makers meant they worked in an entirely different way from both their French predecessors and the Hollywood auteurs so admired by the *Cahiers* critics.

Jean-Paul Belmondo as
Michel Poiccard on the
streets of Paris

# french new wave background

Finally, the late 1950s saw the emergence of a 'youth culture', epitomised by Elvis Presley and rock and roll. It was perhaps not surprising then that the energy for a new approach to film-making should come from young directors in their late twenties and early thirties.

One of the first New Wave films was François Truffaut's debut film, *Les quatre cents coups* (*The 400 Blows*). Made and released in 1959, it became the surprise hit of the year. Yearning to follow his friend's success Jean-Luc Godard proposed four ideas for films to producer Georges de Beauregard. *A bout de souffle* was chosen, possibly because the idea for the script came from François Truffaut, who had already proved his capability. In order to secure the film's funding Jean-Luc Godard agreed to list Claude Chabrol, who had already been successful in 1959 with *Les Cousins* (*The Cousins*), as 'technical consultant'. However, Claude Chabrol, like François Truffaut, had very little to do with the actual production of *A bout de souffle*.

# the production of
# a bout de souffle

The origins of *A bout de souffle* are slightly mysterious. François Truffaut composed a treatment for the film in 1955–56, supposedly based on a news story he had read. This original treatment is reprinted in Andrew Dudley's book *Breathless*. Jean-Luc Godard used the treatment as the blueprint for his film, although he never produced a shooting script. Instead, the screenplay for the film has been produced in hindsight, as a description of the film's dialogue and action.

Jean-Luc Godard has described how he wrote the scenes for the film the night before filming them:

> I had written the first scene (Jean Seberg on the Champs-Elysées), and for the rest I had a pile of notes for each scene. I said to myself, this is terrible. I stopped everything. Then I thought: in a single day, if one knows how to go about it, one should be able to complete a dozen takes. Only instead of planning ahead, I shall invent at the last minute. If you know where you're going it ought to be possible.

> This isn't improvisation, but last-minute focusing. Obviously you must have an over-all plan and stick to it; you can modify up to a point, but when shooting begins it should change as little as possible, otherwise it's catastrophic.
>
> *Milne (ed.), 1986, pp. 172–3*

*A bout de souffle* was filmed on location in Paris and Marseilles, between August 17 and September 15 1959. According to *Sight and Sound* in 1960, the budget for the film was 400,000 francs, equivalent to £30,000.

*A bout de souffle* was released in France in March 1960, and was a hit with critics and the public. It was then released with subtitles and a change of title in New York in February 1961 and in England in July 1961. *A bout de souffle* was translated, not particularly accurately, as *Breathless* for the English-speaking market. It has been suggested that 'out of breath' might have better captured the connotations of the French term 'a bout de souffle'.

# key players' biographies

## JEAN SEBERG

Jean Seberg, who stared as the film's lead female character Patricia Franchini, was a well-known American actress. Two years earlier, at the age of nineteen, she had been plucked from obscurity to play the lead role in Otto Preminger's *Saint Joan*. Although she did not receive good reviews for the role, she came to the attention of the *Cahiers* critics, who considered Otto Preminger to be an auteur.

In 1958 Jean Seberg starred in another Preminger film, *Bonjour tristesse*. Jean-Luc Godard describes how he took the inspiration for Jean Seberg's character in *A bout de souffle* from *Bonjour tristesse*:

> For some shots I referred to scenes I remembered from Preminger, Cukor, etc. And the character played by Jean Seberg was a continuation of her role in *Bonjour tristesse*. I could have taken the last shot of Preminger's film and started after dissolving to a title, 'Three Years Later'.
>
> *Milne (ed.), 1986, p. 173*

# biographies  background

The success of *A bout de souffle* turned Jean Seberg into an icon of the era, as women copied the style of her short cropped haircut. However, Jean Seberg's career after *A bout de souffle* was mixed. She worked in both the US and Europe, on films as varied as *Lilith* (1964), *Paint Your Wagon* and *Airport* (both 1969).

Unfortunately, Jean Seberg's film career was often overshadowed by her private life. She had three failed marriages and many public affairs. She had been involved with the National Association for the Advancement of Colored People in the US since the age of fourteen and was committed to the Civil Rights movement. In the late 1960s Jean Seberg became linked with the Black Panther Party, and this brought her to the attention of the FBI. She was also having an affair at the time with a militant leader of the Malcolm X Foundation. The FBI wanted to discredit Jean Seberg, and when she became pregnant they spread rumours that the father of her child was a Black Panther. The idea of a white movie star with a black militant during the period of the American Civil Rights unrest in the late 1960s was very damaging. Jean Seberg's baby was born prematurely and died. Jean Seberg never really recovered from the loss; she became dependent on alcohol and barbiturates. In August 1979 Jean Seberg disappeared. She was found dead ten days later in her car in a Paris backstreet.

## JEAN-PAUL BELMONDO

Jean Seberg's co-star, Jean-Paul Belmondo, has had a successful film career in his native France. Jean-Paul Belmondo trained as an actor at the Conservatoire where he caused uproar in his final exams. He chose a 'shocking' piece to perform, and the judges, who thought he was mocking them, only awarded him third prize, to much 'booing' from the audience. He started work as a comedy actor on the stage and then moved into film. Jean-Paul Belmondo played the central role in one of Jean-Luc Godard's first short films, *Charlotte et son Jules* (*Charlotte and her Jules*) (1959), although in this film his voice was dubbed by Jean-Luc Godard. Jean-Paul Belmondo then went on to play the character Laszlo Kovacs (the alias used by Belmondo's character in *A bout de souffle*) in Claude Chabrol's film *A double tour* (1959).

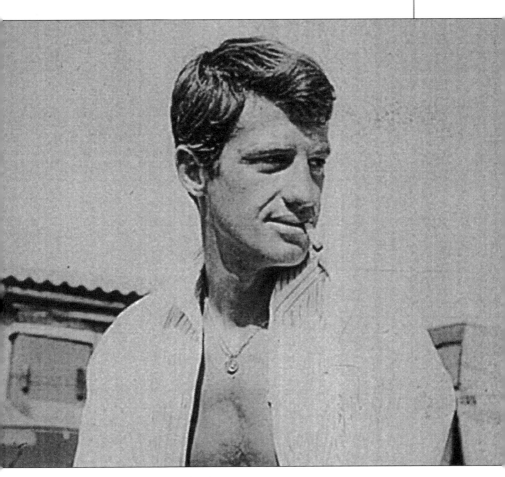

Jean-Paul Belmondo became
a star of French cinema after
the success of *A bout de souffle*

# biographies  background

the best young actor in Europe

Jean-Paul Belmondo's portrayal of the antihero Michel Poiccard in *A bout de souffle* made him an international star. The 'Personality of the Month' feature in October 1960's *Films and Filming* described how:

> A few months ago the name of Jean-Paul Belmondo meant little either at the French box-office or with the French papers. To them he was just another of the multitude of young actors that had been emerging over the past three or four years. Then suddenly, virtually overnight, he found himself a top star with his performance in *A bout de souffle* and during past months his name has never been out of the French film magazines.

By 1964 Jean-Paul Belmondo had won three French 'Oscars'. Henry Fonda named him as one of the three best actors in the world, and the director Peter Brook described him as the best young actor in Europe. Jean-Paul Belmondo worked with Jean-Luc Godard again on two films, *Une Femme est une femme* (*A Woman Is a Woman*) (1961) and *Pierrot le fou* (*Pierrot Goes Wild*) (1965). However, he moved more and more towards working in the French popular cinema. Jean-Paul Belmondo has appeared in over seventy films in his career to date but as most of these have not been widely distributed outside of France, much of his work has not been seen by English-speaking audiences. Generally, the only French films distributed internationally are those that can be classified as art cinema. Like Jean Seberg then, Jean-Paul Belmondo remains best remembered internationally for his role in *A bout de souffle*.

## RAOUL COUTARD

Just as important as the contribution of the two stars and Jean-Luc Godard to the success of *A bout de souffle* was the work of cinematographer, Raoul Coutard. Owing to his radical plans for filming *A bout de souffle* Jean-Luc Godard did not initially want to work with Raoul Coutard whom he did not know. However, the producer Georges de Beauregard insisted that Raoul Coutard be used, as he had worked with him previously on some documentaries. This decision had a strong impact on the subsequent look of many of the New Wave films as Raoul Coutard worked extensively with both Jean-Luc Godard and François Truffaut.

After serving in the French army in Vietnam for eleven years Raoul Coutard became a photojournalist. He stayed on in Vietnam and produced photographs for *Paris Match* and *Life*. Working in Saigon he met the influential photojournalist Ernst Haas. Raoul Coutard's experience as a photojournalist had a significant effect on the later style of 'realism' prevalent in the cinematography of films such as *A bout de souffle* (see Style: Cinematography).

Raoul Coutard left Vietnam in the mid 1950s and returned to his native Paris. Here he produced press photographs, worked on a French form of 'photo comic-strips' and ended up as a cameraman on feature documentaries. However, his first big break in film-making was working on *A bout de souffle*.

Raoul Coutard formed a strong partnership with Jean-Luc Godard and the pair eventually worked together on seventeen films. In an interview in *American Cinematographer* in March 1997 Raoul Coutard expressed the view that: 'the only one who really wanted to change film-making, the only real revolutionary, was Jean-Luc Godard.'

Overall, Raoul Coutard has worked on over eighty films in his career. In 1997 he was honoured for his achievements with the American Society of Cinematographers International Award.

## JEAN-LUC GODARD

*A bout de souffle* also proved to be the springboard for the successful film-making career of Jean-Luc Godard. In an article in *Sight and Sound* in January 1998, Michael Temple stated:

> Jean-Luc Godard is one of those mythical figures of film culture, like Eisenstein, Welles or Pasolini – whose work is almost impossible to separate from the legends, distortions and fierce loyalties inspired by the mention of their names. Like him or loathe him, Godard is indispensable to our understanding of what cinema is, what it has been and what it might yet be in the next century.

Jean-Luc Godard was born on 3 December 1930 in Paris. His father was a Swiss doctor and his mother came from a rich Parisian banking family. He

rather a 'wild child'

was the second of four children. Although a French citizen by birth, he was naturalised as a Swiss citizen during the Second World War and he has kept his dual citizenship throughout his life.

Jean-Luc Godard spent his school years in Switzerland, but moved to Paris when he was nineteen to study for a degree in ethnology at the Sorbonne. As a student in Paris he began to develop his love of the cinema as he attended the cinéclubs in the Latin Quarter and Henri Langlois's Cinémathèque. It was here that Jean-Luc Godard took in much of the history of the cinema and struck up friendships with François Truffaut, André Bazin, Claude Chabrol, Eric Rohmer and Jacques Rivette to form the nucleus of *Cahiers du cinéma* and the French New Wave.

In the early 1950s Jean-Luc Godard began to write for *La Gazette du cinéma* and then for *Cahiers du cinéma*, he also acted in some of his friends' early short films. During this period he was rather a 'wild child'. He reportedly stole money from various friends and family to support himself, and his relationship with his father became more and more troubled. Jean-Luc Godard's mother secured him a job with the Swiss national television network in 1952, and then found him work again as a construction labourer on a Swiss dam in early 1954.

Jean-Luc Godard used the money earned from this job to finance his first film, a short documentary on the building of the dam, entitled *Opération béton* (literally, 'Concrete Operation'). The construction company liked the film, shot in the professional standard of 35mm, and paid Jean-Luc Godard for it. He spent his profits on making his next short film, *Une Femme coquette* (*A Flirtatious Woman*).

Jean-Luc Godard's early success was overshadowed by the death of his mother in a motorcycle accident in 1954. He was already cut off from most of his family, and from now on he dedicated himself to a life in the cinema. In 1957 Jean-Luc Godard made his first short feature film with a professional cast, *Tous les garçons s'appellent Patrick* (*All the Boys are Called Patrick*). Claude Chabrol got Jean-Luc Godard a job in the publicity department of Twentieth Century Fox, and while here he made another two short films: *Une histoire d'eau* (*A Story of Water*) (1958) was a collaborative film with François Truffaut, while

*Charlotte et son Jules* was made with the then little-known actor Jean-Paul Belmondo.

François Truffaut's commercial and critical success with *Les quatre cents coups* in 1959 inspired Jean-Luc Godard to attempt his first full feature and:

> an opportunity came knocking that would permanently alter the course of Jean-Luc Godard's life, and change the face of the cinema forever, not only in France and the United States, but throughout the entire international cinema community.
>
> *Dixon, 1997, p. 13*

*A bout de souffle* catapulted Jean-Luc Godard to fame and he soon became one of the best-known directors of the New Wave. However, his career has taken an unusual and often controversial path, and he has not made anything quite as commercially popular as *A bout de souffle* since.

After *A bout de souffle*, Jean-Luc Godard's next film was *Le Petit Soldat* (The Little Soldier). Made in 1960, it dealt controversially with the French/Algerian war and was banned until 1963. This meant that the next Jean-Luc Godard film seen by audiences was the 1961 *Une Femme est une femme* in which the film-maker played with the conventions of the musical, much as the conventions of the gangster movie had been experimented with in *A bout de souffle*. From 1960 to 1966 Jean-Luc Godard made a number of films which varied in their critical and commercial success, including *Vivre sa vie* (1962, *My Life to Live*), *Les Carabiniers* (1963, *The Riflemen; The Soldiers*), *Le Mépris* (1963), *Bande à part* (1964), *Une Femme mariée* (1964, *A Married Woman*), *Alphaville* (1965) and *Pierrot le fou* (1965). Jean-Luc Godard then started to move further and further away from the mainstream. As Julia Lesage explains (1979, p. 5):

> From 1966 on, Godard's statements to the press took on an increasingly politicized tone, as did his films. He chafed at the ideological and financial strictures of the film industry, the French governmental system of film finance and censorship, and the

the politics of class struggle

Ministry of Culture itself. [...] Godard shot *Made in the USA* and *Deux ou trois choses que je sais d'elle* [*Two or Three Things I Know about Her*] in the summer of 1966, and these as well as his two films completed in 1967 contain trenchant critiques, still from within a bourgeois intellectual framework, of capitalist social and economic structures and the personal relations which they engender. Because of his own intellectual and political development, Godard, of all the New Wave film-makers, would be the most receptive to and the most affected by the civil rebellion in France in 1968.

In May 1968 there was massive civil unrest in France with anti-government demonstrations demanding better pay, better working conditions and better education for all. By this time Jean-Luc Godard was involved in the politics of class struggle. While his old compatriots of the New Wave were becoming subsumed within the more conventional, popular French cinema, Jean-Luc Godard was rejecting everything about traditional film-making, distribution and exhibition. Between 1969 and 1973 Jean-Luc Godard worked closely with Jean-Pierre Gorin, producing films that were politically militant, in both their content and style. *British Sounds* for example, made for London Weekend Television in 1969 but never screened, dealt with issues on the factory floor in long continuous tracking shots which travel one way across the factory floor, and then back again in the opposite direction.

In 1974 Jean-Luc Godard shifted into working with video on a number of collaborative pieces with Anne-Marie Miéville. They established the Sonimage film and video production studio in Grenoble, producing work such as *Numéro deux* (*Number Two*) (1975). Throughout the 1980s and 1990s Jean-Luc Godard returned to working in the cinema with films such as *Sauve qui peut* (1980, *Everyman for Himself*), *Passion* (1982), *Nouvelle Vague* (*New Wave*) (1990) and *Forever Mozart* (1996). He also worked on the mammoth project of putting together *Histoire(s) du cinéma*, a montage of images in eight parts, celebrating the history of cinema from Jean-Luc Godard's unique perspective.

# director as auteur

Jean-Luc Godard is a challenging film-maker with a vast portfolio spanning forty years. Some critics dislike much of his work, dismissing it as pretentious, self-indulgent and over-intellectual. Others believe Jean-Luc Godard to have been one of the most important and influential directors of the twentieth century, shaping the medium of cinema by pushing at its boundaries from the 'outside'.

So, is Jean-Luc Godard an auteur? The question turns full circle. As one of the writers involved in the development of the *politique des auteurs* at *Cahiers du cinéma*, Jean-Luc Godard can perhaps be assessed as one of the cinema's great auteurs. In fact, Jean-Luc Godard is possibly one of the 'purest' of auteurs. Because he has spent much of his career working outside the confines of the organised film industry he has been able to pursue his own ideas, and experiment with film language in his own unique way.

However, the auteur approach is not that simple. Indeed, it is a theory that created its own intense theoretical debate. The origins of the *politique des auteurs* can be found in a seminal article written by Alexandre Astruc in 1948. In 'The birth of a new avant-garde: La caméra-stylo' he put forward the view that:

> the cinema is quite simply becoming a means of expression, just as all the other arts have been before it, and in particular painting and the novel. After having been successively a fairground attraction, an amusement analogous to boulevard theatre, or a means of preserving the images of an era, it is gradually becoming a language. By language, I mean a form in which and by which an artist can express his thoughts, however abstract they may be, or translate his obsessions exactly as he does in the contemporary essay or novel. This is why I would like to call this new age of cinema the age of the *caméra-stylo* (camera-pen).
>
> *printed in Peter Graham (ed.), The New Wave, Critical Landmarks, pp. 17–18*

Alexandre Astruc's call to 'transform the cinema' was taken up in the *politique des auteurs*, in the *Cahiers* critics' analyses of Hollywood

# director as auteur

films and film-makers, and in their own films of the New Wave. Essays in *Cahiers* identified certain directors such as Howard Hawks and Alfred Hitchcock as the authors of their films on account of their creative use of film language.

However, the *politique des auteurs* was reformulated in the United States by critic Andrew Sarris as 'the auteur theory'. Outside the cultural context of France the approach created a 'pantheon' of great directors, sidelining those who did not make the 'A list' to an inferior status. This approach has since been heavily criticised.

The arguments surrounding the auteur theory are varied. Those who subscribe to it believe that it offers a way of understanding the whole oeuvre of a director, that it provides an interesting perspective from which to 'read' a film for those who are aware of a director's previous works, and that it assigns to the cinema its rightful status as an 'art form'. Those who disagree argue that the auteur approach tells us nothing, that it is impossible to locate the 'meaning of a film' with the director as sole creator when it is a collaborative medium which employs so many different people in creative roles, and that it merely creates a 'cult of personality'. As film theory has developed over the years, writers have also condemned the auteur theory as 'too prescriptive', arguing that it asserts the film-maker as 'creator of all meaning' and thus denies the work of the spectator in finding their own meaning in the film, dependent on their own unique perception and circumstances. Modern critics also argue that the notion of auteur is now no more than a 'marketing tag', the label of 'the latest Tarantino or Scorsese film' just becomes a way of targeting a film at a specific audience, rather than providing a critical framework for analysing the film.

However, the controversies surrounding the auteur theory can mask its significance. The *politique des auteurs* marked a key moment in film history. It was a founding part of modern film theory, which evolved into the discipline of film studies. The auteur approach is perhaps now best considered as one way in which to approach the study of a film, rather than as a method for deciding whether a particular director is good, bad or indifferent.

When analysing *A bout de souffle* one can see the film as a 'Jean-Luc Godard film'. Although the film is not as stylistically extreme or experimental as his later work it is interesting to consider the origins of some of his later ideas in this, his first film.

Perhaps Jean-Luc Godard can even be considered the most interesting auteur of all. If one returns to Alexandre Astruc's notion of the 'camera pen', Jean-Luc Godard has explored and experimented with the language of the cinema perhaps more than any other film-maker. By working creatively with the tools of his trade: the camera, sound and narrative, he has challenged his spectators to think about, rather than just absorb, his images non-critically.

As Jean-Luc Godard's first film, *A bout de souffle* can also be viewed as central to the rewriting of what a film could be, in terms of its financing, its production, its narrative, its editing, its sound and its images. 'For good and ill *A bout de souffle* is one of the most influential films of our time and belongs with a group of European pictures made between 1958 and 1962 that transformed and renewed the cinema.' (Philip French, *The Observer*, 24 July 1988).

# narrative & form

## film narrative

One of the first, most fundamental questions to consider when starting to analyse the cinema is: why narrative? When the first films of the Lumière brothers were shown they were recordings of real-life events such as a train arriving at a station or workers leaving a factory. Initially, films were screened at fairgrounds or as part of music hall entertainment, and their novelty factor was that no one had ever seen real moving images before 1895. However, it was clear the novelty of the technology would not last for very long.

The recording technology behind the cinema could have been used for many different purposes, for example to document events, or for scientific study. After all, it was Eadweard Muybridge's quest to analyse the movement of animals that first led to the discovery of the technology of the moving image. Film has certainly been used throughout its history for documentaries and news reporting, although these functions have now largely been taken over by television.

However, the most prosperous use of moving-image technology soon became associated with telling stories. The novel and the theatre were already well-established mediums of entertainment at the turn of the twentieth century. The very first narrative films did little more than record tableaus of action, as they would have been played out on the stage. But gradually, over the course of twenty years, the cinema developed its own way of telling stories.

It appears that storytelling is a powerful part of most human societies. From the Bible to the plays of Shakespeare, and even to the way in which we recount the events of our day to friends and family, the form of the story provides us with a way in which to communicate. In a bid to understand the way in which stories function, various theorists have analysed storytelling. One such theorist was the Russian linguist Vladimir

flickering projection of light on a screen

Propp. In the 1920s he analysed Russian folk tales and found that whatever their content they all followed the same basic pattern. His findings thus concluded that there existed certain conventions which structured the way stories were told. These conventions were not written down, as folk tales were most commonly passed on verbally from generation to generation. However, by identifying what the conventions were, Vladimir Propp demonstrated that stories were not just told in a 'haphazard' way but that, like language, they had a basic 'grammar'.

Vladimir Propp's work has been very influential in film studies. As a theoretical discipline, the study of film seeks to understand how the flickering projection of light on a screen creates meaning which millions of spectators around the world understand. Analysing the structure of narrative is an essential part of this.

When discussing narrative it is necessary to understand the meaning of the word as it is used in film studies. Narrative does not refer to the story. The content, or story, of a film is called the plot. Narrative refers to the way in which the story is told. Therefore, the narrative is part of the form, or the structure, of a film. One analogy might be to compare a film with a car. Studying narrative is like studying the components of an engine to understand how it makes a car work. Studying the way in which a story is told holds the key to understanding how we as spectators make sense of the film. That is why film studies concentrates on the narrative structure of a film, rather than on the details of a film's plot.

## THE DEVELOPMENT OF NARRATIVE IN HOLLYWOOD

Throughout its history the cinema has adapted stories from novels, from plays, and even from the Bible. However, the cinema has evolved its own form and language to tell these stories, based on images and sounds that are edited together. The way in which the dominant form of cinema has developed is tied closely to the industrial and economic organisation of Hollywood.

Between 1895 and 1914 the techniques of film-making were being developed in both America and Europe. European countries with strong traditions of film-making included England, France, Germany and Italy. However, the First World War halted film production in Europe, and during this period the American film industry started to dominate world cinema. One reason for this was the sheer size of the American population. Films made in America recouped their production costs at the American domestic box office and then could be sold cheaply around the world, making it difficult for European film-makers to compete financially in their own countries.

As the silent era of film-making came to a close at the end of the 1920s it was the Hollywood studios, with the backing of Wall Street, who could first afford to make the substantial investments needed to wire the studios and the cinemas for sound. Introducing sound to the cinema did not just affect studio and cinema technology. The cinematic 'language' of editing, framing, lighting and acting styles also had to adapt to the new era. As the Hollywood studios held a position of international dominance in the cinema, the language and conventions of sound film-making that Hollywood evolved to suit its purposes became the most influential around the world.

The Hollywood conventions for storytelling in the sound cinema, which became known as Classical Hollywood Narrative evolved over a period of time between the late 1920s and the mid 1930s. As vertically integrated businesses which supplied one of America's key world exports, the studios' main aim was to make money by entertaining people. Therefore, as a narrative formula successful with audiences became established it was consolidated. To understand what it was that *A bout de souffle* did that was so radical in 1959, it is necessary to understand what the Classical Hollywood Narrative conventions were.

## CLASSICAL HOLLYWOOD NARRATIVE

The basic conventions of Classical Hollywood Narrative cinema can be listed as:

- equilibrium, disruption, re-equilibrium
- closure

■ cause and effect

■ role of the protagonist

■ continuity editing

It might seem rather obvious to say that a Classical Hollywood Narrative film has a beginning, a middle and an end. But one has to stop and consider why this is so. The pattern of equilibrium, disruption, re-equilibrium describes the basic structure of a film made in the Classical Hollywood Narrative style. Equilibrium is the state of 'balanced calm' that exists in the world of the characters before the 'events' of the film. A disruption takes place which affects the lives of the characters in some way. The film is then all about how the disruption or problem is solved. Finally, the film ends once a 'balanced equilibrium' is regained.

*Casablanca* provides a good example of a Classical Hollywood Narrative film, made at the height of the studio system in 1942. This film opens with a spinning globe and a voice-over explaining the trail of Second World War refugees who have travelled through Europe and Africa, arriving in Casablanca in the hope of escaping to America. The equilibrium of the world of the characters is shown as they carry on with their daily wartime life. The film concentrates particularly on Rick's café, and the character of Rick, played by the star Humphrey Bogart. The narrative disruption occurs when Ilsa, an old flame of Rick's, arrives in Casablanca with her resistance-leader husband Victor Laslow. Ilsa and Victor need two rare 'letters of transit' to leave Casablanca, and Rick has them hidden in his café. The lives of the characters are thrown into turmoil as Rick and Ilsa rekindle their love and plot how to escape to America. The film works through all of the problems thrown up by the narrative until all is finally resolved in the last scene at the airport, when Rick sends Ilsa off with Victor because he realises that Victor's escape is important to the Allies' war effort. The structuring device of equilibrium, disruption, re-equilibrium which underpins *Casablanca* is powerful because it provides us, as spectators, with expectations of where the narrative will go. This helps us to read the film and understand it, partly because we can predict its parameters. The role of equilibrium, disruption, re-equilibrium might appear obvious, but it

closure ... sends an audience away happy

is only when the device is removed, in a film that has 'no beginning, middle or end', that one can appreciate how difficult it is to understand a film without a conventional structure.

The term closure refers to the way in which a Classical Hollywood Narrative film draws itself to a close. It is similar to re-equilibrium, but specifically describes how all the 'loose ends' of a story are tied together. In a Classical Hollywood Narrative film everything in the narrative is resolved. In *Casablanca* Victor and Ilsa escape and Rick explains why this has to happen. The Nazi officer trying to prevent Victor and Ilsa from leaving is killed. Finally, Rick and his friend the French police officer 'walk off into the mist together', discussing how they too will need to get away from Casablanca. The spectator has also already been shown what happens to the other main characters in the film. Rick sells his café, and his pianist and bar staff are still employed. Closure is a narrative technique which signals the end of a film and sends an audience away happy. This was vital to Hollywood as an entertainment business because the studios wanted the audience to return for more. Hence the ubiquitous Hollywood 'happy ending'.

Cause and effect describes the way in which the individual scenes of a film are 'stitched together'. Every scene in a Classical Hollywood Narrative film is linked and motivated. In *Casablanca* the man who has stolen the letters of transit gives them to Rick for safe keeping. Then, lo and behold, it is Rick's ex-lover who needs the letters, and Rick who thus holds the key to the future for all of the characters. Nothing extraneous is shown or discussed in a Classical Hollywood Narrative film. Everything that is presented to the spectator is there for a narrative reason. This helps guide the spectator in their reading of a film. They don't have to decipher what might be important or relevant from what they see and hear. The sifting has already been done for them. Cause and effect was and is a vital element of the success of Hollywood films, because it makes the narrative so easy to understand.

The role of the protagonist in Classical Hollywood Narrative films, closely linked to the star system, was also a key factor of success. The protagonist is the main character in a narrative film, usually the film's hero and star. In

a coherent time and space

*Casablanca* the protagonist is Rick. The role is played by Humphrey Bogart, who was one of Warner Brothers' leading stars of the time. Most if not all of the events in a Classical Hollywood Narrative film revolve around the protagonist. The narrative disruption affects them, they are linked to the chain of cause and effect and their actions bring about the film's closure. The protagonist also usually occupies a central place in the images of the film. The camera keeps them at the centre of the frame, thus encouraging spectator identification. Classical Hollywood Narrative protagonists are always motivated, so that spectators can understand the cause of their actions, and usually they are 'on the side of the angels', that is, they play the good guy (and invariably they are male). Yet again, the role of the protagonist acts as a guiding force for the spectator who is 'reading' the film. They can identify the protagonist early on and know what to expect from them.

Finally, the continuity editing system evolved as the best way to compensate for the fragmentation of time and space caused by editing. A typical Classical Hollywood Narrative film is made up of well over a thousand shots. Each edit has the potential to disrupt and confuse a spectator, particularly if a section of time is cut out or the location of the action is changed.

The continuity editing system consists of a series of 'unwritten rules' which create a coherent time and space for the diegetic world of the narrative. Spatial continuity is achieved with a variety of techniques. Two basic rules of angle exist to ensure that screen direction is consistent and that cuts are 'smooth'. The 180° rule means that the camera does not cross over an 'imaginary line' drawn between the positions of the actors in a scene when shooting. The 35° rule means that a change in camera angle should always be of more than 35 degrees. Any less than this and, because the change in angle is so small, it looks as though the image has just 'jumped'.

The sequencing and framing of shots is also controlled by the continuity editing system. Each scene needs to start with an establishing shot. Only after this establishing work has been achieved can the camera cut into mid shots and close-ups on the actors and objects significant to the narrative.

During dialogue sequences a pattern of shot/reverse shot is set up. Eyeline-match and match-on-action are two methods that ensure edits are motivated. Because the Hollywood cinema wanted to entertain people first and foremost, it wanted spectators to concentrate on the content of the narrative's story, rather than on the way in which the film had been constructed through its editing. Techniques which motivated and thus made the edits invisible were of great significance for the Classical Hollywood Narrative system.

Overlapping sound is the final spatial continuity editing technique, which works to smooth over potentially disruptive transitions between scenes. Not only does this help to hide the process of editing, it also provides a bridge between two scenes, indicating to the spectator that the place the story has moved to is part of the same continuing narrative world.

All of the above spatial editing techniques are to be found throughout *Casablanca*. The fact that they are meant to make the editing invisible means that they are difficult to spot. When watching the film, a spectator is usually not consciously aware of the editing. They do not have to work hard to construct the narrative space in their mind (as one does when reading a novel), and the film therefore appears, as if by magic, to take place in a seamless three-dimensional diegetic world.

As well as space, editing also constructs the time frame of a film. Nearly all films condense real time into 'reel time', so that narrative events that might take place over a day, a week, a year, or a lifetime, can be shown in ninety minutes. Most films therefore 'cut time out'. To ensure that a spectator is not confused, Classical Hollywood Narrative films usually relay narrative events in a chronological order. When shifts in time, such as flashbacks or flashforwards do occur they are clearly signalled by conventions. For example when Rick and Ilsa's love affair in Paris before the Nazi invasion is shown in *Casablanca* the screen dissolves and tonal changes in the music indicate that the film has 'gone back in time'.

Types of edit also became associated with particular time frames in the Classical Hollywood Narrative cinema to ensure that spectators would understand the temporal logic of a film. Cuts were used within scenes to show continuous time, meaning that within a scene no time was cut out. Fades and dissolves were used between scenes to signal clearly the end of a scene and indicate the passing of time before the next scene. Other editing techniques, such as the iris and the wipe were used less after the silent era. Instead the cut, the fade and the dissolve became the basic punctuation of the Classical Hollywood Narrative cinema, making it easy for spectators all over the world to understand.

The invisible nature of the conventions of the Classical Hollywood Narrative system accounts largely for their power and success as a narrative tool. Just like a quiet, perfectly engineered engine in a top-of-the-range car, the Classical Hollywood Narrative conventions work away in the background, not drawing attention to themselves, but carrying out their job efficiently. The fact that the conventions are so unobtrusive makes the need to study them even more imperative because they implicitly carry much of the ideology of a film (see Contexts) in what appears to be a 'natural' way.

All of these narrative conventions form part of the 'language of the cinema' and thus are part of a film's 'form'. Reading a film is like reading a book. As you read this book your brain is working to decode the shapes of letters on the page, to ascertain the relationship of the letters to each other to create words, and from the words to create sentences. The alphabet, grammar and punctuation enable you to make sense of the shapes on the page. The job is also made easier because your brain has learnt to expect certain combinations of letters, words and grammatical constructs.

These same principles can be applied to the work you do when you are reading a film. Narrative conventions provide a framework for our reading. Expectations of the way a film will begin, progress and end, how it will follow a protagonist and how it will be edited, feed into the pleasure gained from watching and reading a film.

# narrative in a bout de souffle

The Classical Hollywood Narrative system lasted until the mid 1950s. Anti-trust legislation challenged the vertical integration of Hollywood and the studio system started to break down. At the same time a new post-war generation and society was emerging in America and Europe, and this started to influence both the type of films made, and the way in which they were made. If the silent period was the first generation of film-making and Classical Hollywood Narrative cinema was the second generation, then the third generation was about to be born. *A bout de souffle* was made in this context, and it is in this context that any analysis of how its form and narrative work must be made.

Although *A bout de souffle* is not as radical in its narrative structure as Jean-Luc Godard's later films, it certainly provided something different and revolutionary in its day. Jean-Luc Godard claims:

> *A bout de souffle* was the sort of film where anything goes: that was what it was all about. [...] What I wanted was to take a conventional story and remake, but differently, everything the cinema had done. I also wanted to give the feeling that the techniques of film-making had just been discovered or experienced for the first time. The iris-in showed that one could return to the cinema's sources; the dissolve appeared, just once, as though it had just been invented.
>
> *Milne, 1986, p. 173*

*A bout de souffle* does have a narrative plot of sorts. The protagonist, Michel Poiccard, steals a car in Marseilles and heads to Paris to find his American girlfriend Patricia. En route he runs into trouble with the police for speeding and ends up killing one of the policemen. In Paris Michel finds Patricia and attempts to persuade her to go with him to Italy. Patricia is studying at university and trying to establish a career as a journalist. She thinks she may be pregnant with Michel's child, but isn't sure if she loves

The detectives hunting for Michel
Poiccard approach Patricia in
the *New York Herald Tribune* office

lack of a clear, motivated goal

him. Michel has to track down a friend of his to cash a cheque for him before he leaves for Italy. The police are gradually catching up with Michel, and eventually they get to Patricia. Patricia decides to turn Michel in to the police. She tells him what she has done, but he refuses to try to escape. Michel is finally gunned down in the street as Patricia looks on.

This plot forms the basic content of the film. However, Jean-Luc Godard is not really interested in the plot. Instead he is concerned with exploring the ways in which the story can be told. This means the telling of the story is much looser than in a traditional Classical Hollywood Narrative film.

In *Casablanca* the disruption caused by Ilsa and Victor's arrival is clearly defined. The goal of re-equilibrium can only be achieved when Ilsa and Victor escape with the letters of transit after Rick and Ilsa have resolved the problems from their past relationship. In *A bout de souffle* the narrative disruption is not quite as clear. The film opens with Michel at the harbour in Marseilles. He steals a car, although his motive for this is not clear. He then shoots the policeman, but because the spectator has not been given any prior information on Michel's motive for stealing the car, or on his past background, there is no justification given for his extreme action. The shooting does cause a disruption to Michel's life because he has to avoid the police who are pursuing him, but Michel acts as though they are no more than a mild annoyance. Indeed, Michel's primary goal throughout the film seems to revolve more around getting Patricia into bed, than around escaping successfully from the police.

The lack of a clear, motivated goal for the film's narrative means that the film ambles along, often slowly. Neither Patricia nor Michel seem to know what they want, and therefore there are few expectations raised for the spectator as to what the point of re-equilibrium might be. The close of the film perhaps provides a sort of re-equilibrium for the characters. Michel tells Berruti: 'I'm beat, I'm tired, I feel like sleeping.' So it could be said that death provides him with a refuge from life. Likewise, Patricia tells Michel: 'because I am mean to you, ... it proves that I am not in love with you.' As she turns away from Michel as he lays dead on the street, she may feel at peace with herself, secure in the belief that her actions were correct. However, it is hard for the spectator to know how to feel about Michel's death and Patricia's betrayal. Because the film does not use the familiar pattern of equilibrium, disruption, re-equilibrium the spectator feels ambivalent about how the film ends.

The closure of *A bout de souffle* caused problems for Jean-Luc Godard. As he explains:

> What caused me a lot of trouble was the end. Should the hero die? To start with, I intended to do the opposite of, say, *The Killing*: the gangster would win and leave for Italy with his money. But as an anti-convention it was too conventional [...] Finally, I decided that as my avowed ambition was to make an ordinary gangster film, I had no business deliberately contradicting the genre: he must die.
>
> *Milne,1986, p. 174*

The death of Michel does provide narrative closure for *A bout de souffle* in one sense: after all, the police have got their man and the relationship between Michel and Patricia is irrevocably finished. However, at the same time, the film denies full closure. As Michel dies he makes faces at Patricia and then says: 'C'est vraiment dégueulasse', which is translated in the latest version of the English language subtitles as: 'It's a real scumbag.' Patricia, who all through the film has asked Michel for translations of French phrases, asks the policemen Inspector Vital: 'What did he say?' Vital replies: 'Une dégueulasse' (You're a real scumbag). Patricia stares out at the camera and says finally: 'What's a scumbag?' then she turns and walks away.

This ending to the film goes against the conventions of the Classical Hollywood Narrative cinema. It denies a neat re-equilibrium. Patricia has misunderstood Michel's last words to her, and Michel has died misunderstood. In Classical Hollywood narratives everything was always explained so as to be understood, both by the characters and by the spectators. The ending of *A bout de souffle* is perhaps a little more 'realistic': after all, real lives and real relationships do not get neatly closed off. But like Patricia, the spectator is left a little confused. In cinematic terms, the technique Jean-Luc Godard uses draws attention to the very

Michel's actions appear unmotivated

nature of the convention of closure by making the spectator consider their own expectations of film endings.

Jean-Luc Godard does present the plot of *A bout de souffle* in a chronological order. However, he discards the convention of cause and effect. Cause and effect makes traditional Hollywood films appear to be tightly constructed because nothing extraneous to the goal of achieving re-equilibrium is included and so every scene has a clear purpose. In *A bout de souffle*, partly because the goal of re-equilibrium is less clearly defined, many of Michel's actions, and thus many of the scenes, appear to be unmotivated and unrelated to the rest of the film.

When Michel first arrives in Paris after he has shot the policeman he is shown doing various things before he finds Patricia. First, Michel goes to a phone booth. He puts a coin into the phone slot, but does not make his call successfully. He then has trouble retrieving his money and slams the side of the phone. Michel spends a lot of time in the film trying to reach his friend Berruti on the telephone, but is nearly always unsuccessful. In Classical Hollywood Narrative cinema a phone call would not be shown unless it had a direct effect on the plot, for example in *Casablanca* when Captain Renault phones the German officer to warn him that Victor Laslow is on his way to the airport.

After Michel's unsuccessful phone call he buys a newspaper. He then goes to Patricia's hotel and steals the key because Patricia is not in. He is seen briefly in Patricia's room, and then he goes into a café, where he orders ham and eggs. He tells the waitress he is going to buy a newspaper and leaves the café. He is seen with a newspaper, which he uses to clean his shoes and then throws away. Next he goes up to the apartment of another female friend. We never learn her name, although she is seen once more later in the film, when Michel and Patricia are on their way to meet Berruti. Michel and the girl talk about working in cinema and television and he asks her for money. She tells him she does not have the 5,000 francs he needs, but he does steal some money from her purse while she is getting dressed. Michel leaves her and goes into a travel agency to find his friend Monsieur Tolmatchoff, but yet again he is thwarted because Tolmatchoff is not in. All of this action is inconsequential to the plot, and would never have been

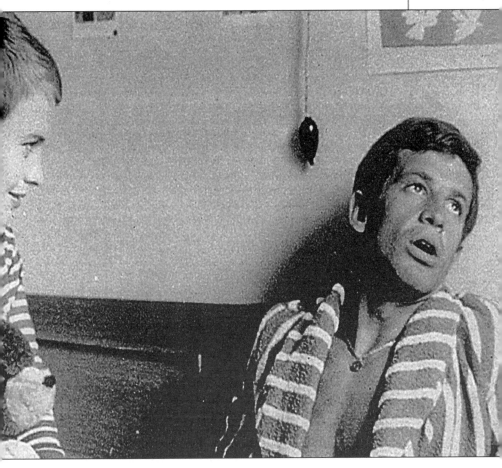

Michel and Patricia spend a long
time just talking and playing games
with each other

a single scene lasts for twenty-five minutes

included in a Classical Hollywood Narrative film; instead Michel would have been shown going directly to speak to Patricia, which is what he does next.

The inclusion of all of this 'extra' action slows down the progression of the film and makes it harder for the spectator to 'read'. In a traditional Hollywood film everything was relevant and therefore the spectator was guided easily through the film. In *A bout de souffle* the spectator has to do more work to differentiate what might be relevant, and what is not. What the spectator does experience instead is a sense of Michel's frustration at not being in control of events, something which affects his standing as a protagonist.

The chain of cause and effect in *A bout de souffle* is weak throughout the film. However, there is one particular scene in which Jean-Luc Godard really departed from the Classical Hollywood Narrative conventions of his day. At the centre of *A bout de souffle* is a single scene that lasts for nearly twenty-five minutes. It begins when Patricia returns to her hotel room after her meeting with the journalist. She finds that her key is missing from the front desk, and goes into her room to find Michel there.

During the scene Michel tries to convince Patricia to go to Rome with him. He also constantly tries to persuade her to sleep with. He says: 'I want to sleep with you because you're beautiful'. She replies: 'No, I'm not'. He says: 'Then, because you're ugly'. To which Patricia asks: 'It's the same?'

Patricia tells Michel she is pregnant and says: 'I only want to know what you'll say'. She is preoccupied with working out if they love each other. 'I wish we were Romeo and Juliet ... You see, you said last night, in the car, you couldn't live without me. But you can. Romeo couldn't live without Juliet, but you can, you can!'

In between their conversations Michel and Patricia play games. They pull faces at each other and in the mirror. They try on each other's clothes, and endlessly move around Patricia's apartment. They discuss the music Patricia plays on her record player and the work of writers:

Patricia

    Do you know William Faulkner?

their conversation goes on, round and round

```
Michel
    No, who is it? You've slept with him?
Patricia
    He's a novelist that I like ... You've read
    The Wild Palms? ... Listen, the last sentence
    is beautiful. 'Between grief and nothing I
    will take grief.'
```

Patricia asks Michel what he would choose. He asks her to show him her toes, and then says:

```
    Grief is idiotic; I'd choose nothingness.
```

And so their conversation goes on, round and round, with very little purpose. They do eventually sleep together, but other than this, the scene does not do anything to further their relationship. The sequence stands disconnected from the rest of the film. Although Michel makes frequent phone calls during the scene, none of which are successful, it is almost as if the 'plot' where Michel is on the run from the police has been suspended. The lack of a strong chain of cause and effect makes the film appear to be rather casual and fragmented. As cause and effect was, and is, such a familiar convention in traditional narrative cinema, its absence challenges spectators to consider and question their own expectations of narrative.

Jean-Luc Godard also asks the spectator of *A bout de souffle* to consider the nature of the protagonist. In Classical Hollywood Narrative cinema the protagonist was crucial to the success of a film. The protagonist, clearly identifiable as the star, would be in control of the film's events, be linked to the chain of cause and effect, and their actions would bring about re-equilibrium and closure. The fact that the spectator would generally experience events from the protagonist's point of view was key to the pleasure of watching a film.

Although it might appear that Michel is the obvious protagonist of *A bout de souffle*, closer analysis reveals a more complex structure within the film. Michel is certainly the character that we follow for the first quarter of the film. It is his action of killing the policeman that essentially forms the film's

Michel is not in control of his own destiny

narrative disruption, and it is his quest to get his money and persuade Patricia to go to Italy that forms the basis of the film's plot. However, Michel is not a 'classic' Hollywood protagonist like his hero Humphrey Bogart, whom he admires and mimics throughout the film.

The actor Jean-Paul Belmondo who plays Michel was relatively unknown when *A bout de souffle* was made (see Background: Key players' biographies), whereas Jean Seberg who plays Patricia was well known from her starring role in Otto Preminger's *Saint Joan* (1957). Also, the character of Michel is not in control of his own destiny. Humphrey Bogart makes all of the decisions in *Casablanca*, eventually outwitting the Nazis, whereas Michel is constantly frustrated by his inability to get through to people to sort out the money he needs. Neither does Michel bring about the film's closure. It is Patricia's action that seals Michel's fate. All he does is decide to give up.

The fact that Michel is not a classic protagonist is also illustrated by his absence from parts of the film. Humphrey Bogart is present in virtually every scene in *Casablanca*, but in *A bout de souffle* the camera leaves Michel behind and follows Patricia when she goes to meet with her journalist friend Van Doude, when she goes to the press conference and when she goes to phone the police to inform on Michel. Michel lacks the privileged position and knowledge usually held by the protagonist and thus he is essentially 'weakened'.

The fragmentation of the role of protagonist between Michel and Patricia creates a rather 'alienating' effect for the spectator, which can perhaps explain why spectators often say they do not actually care about what happens to Michel and Patricia at the end of the film.

The concept of dramatic alienation stems from the dramatist Bertolt Brecht (1898–1956) who believed that spectators should be distanced from the events of a narrative so that they could critically analyse the political themes being played out in a drama. Jean-Luc Godard employs a similar technique in *A bout de souffle* but rather than alienate the spectator to make them aware of political themes he uses alienating techniques to make them more aware of the narrative conventions employed in the cinema.

Godard challenges conventional narrative techniques

Throughout *A bout de souffle* Jean-Luc Godard's narrative techniques draw attention to the conventions of equilibrium, disruption, re-equilibrium, closure, cause and effect and the role of the protagonist. Raised awareness of the conventions, caused by the departure from them, means that attention is drawn towards the enunciator and the process of enunciation. In Classical Hollywood Narrative cinema the enunciation of the plot was usually effaced. This means that the techniques that told or 'narrated' the story were made 'invisible' because everything from editing to camera movement was motivated by the events of the narrative. The spectator was therefore not aware of the narrator, instead the story appeared to miraculously unfold on the screen, something which was key to the pleasure of spectators.

Jean-Luc Godard challenges conventional narrative techniques in *A bout de souffle* and in so doing makes the spectator aware of his presence as a film-maker. Jean-Luc Godard's techniques can be related directly to the *politique des auteurs* (see Background): the call of the *Cahiers du cinéma* writers for the recognition of the creative role of the film-maker. In this sense Jean-Luc Godard can be called an auteur, because the spectator is made aware of his 'signature' as the film's author.

However, Jean-Luc Godard's creative play with the conventions of narrative also emphasises the role and the work of the film spectator. When the sacrosanct conventions of cause and effect, closure and protagonist are tinkered with, the spectator becomes aware of just how much they normally rely on them. Jean-Luc Godard's foregrounding of narrative techniques thus draws attention to the active process of reading a film. Film spectators might appear to be passive, 'absorbing' the events played out on the screen, but actually they are actively engaged in decoding events which have been constructed from the language of the cinema.

Jean-Luc Godard took the accepted conventions of narrative and held a mirror up to them in *A bout de souffle*. The reflection pushed the cinema into a new era of self-awareness and 'maturity', allowing it to address spectators in a new way. Because of this *A bout de souffle* can rightfully be regarded as a key film in the development of the cinema.

# style

Film style is difficult to define. Style is usually understood to refer to the visual and aural elements of a film. However, style can also refer to the narrative structure of a film. The narrative style of *A bout de souffle* has already been described as 'loose' and 'casual' (see Narrative & Form).

## classical hollywood narrative style

A film's style is constructed from mise-en-scène, cinematography, sound and editing. In the Classical Hollywood Narrative cinema film style was subservient to the narrative: its job was to 'serve' the needs of the narrative. It was never meant to draw attention to itself for its own sake.

In looking at continuity editing (see Narrative & Form) we saw how techniques such as eyeline-match, match-on-action and overlapping sound were used in Classical Hollywood Narrative cinema to 'smooth over' editing joins to mask the potentially disruptive force of editing from one shot to another. In the same way techniques were also employed to 'hide' the construction of a film – mise-en-scène, cinematography and sound – so that the narrative could take pride of place in the spectator's attention. Hollywood developed this system in the commercial era of the studio system, firm in the belief that audiences wanted good stories and stars, and were not interested in the intricacies of set design, camera movement or soundtrack composition.

*Casablanca* provides a clear example of the subservience and functionality of film style in the Classical Hollywood Narrative period. The film's mise-en-scène (all of the elements placed in front of the camera during filming including set design, lighting design, costume design, make-up and acting style) is made up only of elements necessary to the narrative. *Casablanca* was filmed entirely on a set. The sets for the café and the market were designed to look as though they could be in north Africa in 1940.

hardly aware of the camera as mediator

The characters' costumes represent something of who they are. Throughout most of the film Rick wears the smart attire of a bar owner, Captain Renault wears his police uniform and Victor wears a white suit, suitable for his representation as the heroic resistance fighter. Ilsa's glamorous clothes are perhaps less functional for someone on the run from the Nazis, but the Hollywood star system meant Ingrid Bergman's costumes would have been accepted as appropriate for the leading lady.

Lighting, as a component of both mise-en-scène and cinematography is again functional and consistent in *Casablanca*. The characters and action are lit so that the spectator can see what is happening. There are no extreme contrasts of light to draw attention to the lighting itself.

The film's cinematography (everything to do with the camera including film stock, film speed, focus, framing and camera movement) also serves the narrative. There are no spectacular camera movements in the film, the camera just keeps subtly re-framing to follow the action in a non-intrusive way. The spectator is hardly aware of the camera as mediator at all.

Likewise, the soundtrack almost 'quietly does its job in the background', if that isn't a contradiction in terms. The music, sound effects and dialogue of *Casablanca* have a powerful effect on the spectator's reading of the film, particularly in the way they cue the emotions of the film's narrative. However, when watching the film the spectator is barely conscious of when music and sound effects are faded in and out to do their work because sound is maintained at a consistent level. An unwritten hierarchy of sound, which dictates that music gradually fades down as a character starts to speak, exists and is accepted in the world of the Classical Hollywood Narrative film.

# style of a bout de souffle

When he made *A bout de souffle* Jean-Luc Godard challenged every aspect of traditional narrative film style, creating his own fresh style, full of energy and vitality. The force and impact of *A bout de souffle*'s style can still be felt when watching the film today, as Mark Kermode describes on the inside cover of the VHS video version of the film released in the UK in 1993:

> Yet watching *A bout de souffle* again, against the frequently dreary background of formulaic nineties' cinema the prime response which the film elicits is not intellectual or critical, but visceral; a simple joy at the sheer bloody-minded vitality of the piece. Although the word 'insolent' is frequently used to describe Jean-Luc Godard's use of dislocatory jump-cuts, the adjective precisely captures the rebellious flavour of the entire film, which brims with an ironically naive exuberance. Many celluloid 'milestones' overturn cinematic conventions simply to become unwatchable time-pieces, but *A bout de souffle* seems perversely to have improved with age. [...] The film has lost none of its surging power.

The style of *A bout de souffle* can be related directly to its thematic concerns. Two thematic strands can be identified within the film. The first is the way it deals with social and cultural fragmentation, and the second is the film's concern with the very nature of film. These two 'themes' weave their way through Jean-Luc Godard's construction of the film.

## MISE-EN-SCÈNE

The mise-en-scène of *A bout de souffle* is essentially naturalistic by virtue of the fact that the film was shot entirely on location. The film starts at the port in Marseilles and then moves to Paris. When Michel first meets up with Patricia they stroll along the Champs Elysées. Many of the passers-by look on in surprise, acknowledging the fact that the scene between Patricia and Michel is being filmed. However, this is not a documentary, and it would appear that the passers-by are a mixture of 'real people' and extras. After Michel has left Patricia he is approached by a young girl who tries to sell him a copy of *Cahiers du cinéma*, very much an in-joke for Jean-Luc Godard and his friends.

The film makes use of a wide variety of locations. The streets of Paris are viewed from the numerous car journeys Michel makes, and Orly airport is visited when Patricia goes to interview the novelist Parvulesco. All of the interior locations, such as Patricia's hotel room and the restaurant where she meets her journalist friend are also real places.

The type of cameras and film stock available to Jean-Luc Godard meant that he could film on location, reducing his shooting costs and enabling him to achieve the look for the film he desired. Most Classical Hollywood Narrative films were filmed on constructed sets because this allowed the studios to manage production effectively. The use of locations by Jean-Luc Godard and the other French New Wave film-makers created a fresh look for their films, one that was perhaps more 'realistic'.

The French New Wave film-makers were not, however, the first to use real locations for their work. André Bazin, the founder of *Cahiers du cinéma*, wrote at length about the work of Italian neo–realist film-makers such as Roberto Rossellini and Vittorio De Sica who produced narrative films on the streets of devastated Europe in the late 1940s. The influence of neo-realism on the French New Wave is evident in both the style of the mise-en-scène and the cinematography adopted.

However, one cannot simply say that the mise-en-scène of *A bout de souffle* is 'realistic', just because Jean-Luc Godard chooses to shoot in real locations rather than on a studio set. As a film-maker Jean-Luc Godard still actively chooses what to place in front of the camera. Therefore the film does not provide a straightforward 'true' image of 1959 Parisian life, rather it is a mediation of Jean-Luc Godard's view of Paris. There is no such thing as reality in the cinema, only the image of reality constructed by the film-maker. Even though Jean-Luc Godard was filming on the streets one senses that he enjoyed contriving the action which takes place, for example when a man is knocked down by a car as Michel walks past. Location filming may

# in a bout de souffle style

the light keeps changing

have produced a new stylistic 'look' for a film such as *A bout de souffle* but Jean-Luc Godard was not aiming to produce a new form of realism.

The method of location filming employed in *A bout de souffle* had an impact on the film's lighting style. Jean-Luc Godard uses natural light throughout most of the film, and because he and cinematographer Raoul Coutard were not setting up specific lighting designs for each shot the lighting is often rather 'patchy' and thus 'noticeable'. When Michel goes to the travel agency to meet his friend Tolmatchoff the scene is filmed in one long tracking shot. As the two characters walk through different parts of the travel agency the quality and intensity of the light keeps changing, from the darker location of corridors through to the bright sunshine streaming in through the windows as they stand in the foyer. In a scene later in the film, when Michel and Patricia run off through a passageway to avoid paying a taxi driver, the screen virtually goes black as no artificial light is used at all to film in a dark alley.

In another scene Jean-Luc Godard rejects the convention of tonal/temporal consistency. When Michel shoots the policeman it appears to be broad daylight. However, after the shooting Michel is seen running across a field and suddenly the light is much darker and it seems to be almost dusk. This is not a 'continuity mistake'. Jean-Luc Godard combines the tonal contrast in lighting with a sudden shift in the volume and tempo of the music on the soundtrack, thus drawing the spectator's attention to both lighting and sound. This sudden cutting of time, from daylight to dusk, makes no logical sense. However, it does fit with the many stylistic jumps in time Jean-Luc Godard creates through his editing technique.

Not only did Jean-Luc Godard choose to experiment with location filming and lighting, he also explored the stylistic use of costumes, make-up and props in the mise-en-scène of *A bout de souffle*. Throughout the film Michel dresses in a pseudo-gangster style as he plays out the role of a gangster. In the opening shot of *A bout de souffle* the camera slowly pans up Michel's body to reveal him smoking a cigarette with a trilby hat pulled down over his face. He mutters: 'So I'm a sonofabitch' and then rubs his thumb across his lips slowly, in a Bogart-style gesture.

The idea of role-playing is extended when Patricia and Michel swap clothes. During the long scene in Patricia's apartment, Michel puts on Patricia's striped dressing gown and Patricia wears Michel's white shirt. In one shot she also puts on Michel's hat and places one of his cigarettes between her fingers as she shuts her eyes and tries to make 'everything go very black'.

Just as Jean-Luc Godard consciously experiments with the conventions of narrative in *A bout de souffle*, so he also explores the way film actors play roles through the physical attributes of their costumes and props. This exploration also feeds through into the way Jean-Luc Godard approaches acting style within the film. By 1959 the 'old Hollywood' acting style employed by stars such as Humphrey Bogart, who pretty much played out his star image in all of his films, had been replaced by the new style of 'method acting' made popular by young actors such as James Dean and Marlon Brando. Although Jean-Paul Belmondo was hailed as the French Marlon Brando after the success of *A bout de souffle* this probably had more to do with the rebellious nature of the character of Michel than with his 'role-playing' acting style.

The looser structure of *A bout de souffle*, brought about by the more casual pattern of cause and effect (see Narrative & Form), means that much of the film's dialogue appears to be improvised. For example in the scene in her apartment Patricia says: 'Last night, I was furious. Now, I don't know, it doesn't matter. No, I'm thinking about nothing. (*leaning up and supporting her chin with her hand*). I'd like to think of something ... (she looks back at Michel) ... but I can't.' However, none of the dialogue in the film was actually improvised. Raoul Coutard, the film's cinematographer explains:

> because the Eclair Cameflex [the type of camera used] was neither silent nor crystal-controlled, the entire film had to be dubbed in postproduction. If you look at the film closely you'll notice that the rhythm of the actors' speech is peculiar, and there's a pause between lines. That's because all of the dialogue was spoken by Jean-Luc during each shot, and the actor would then repeat each of his phrases.
>
> *Bergery, 1997*

# in a bout de souffle style

While the acting style throughout *A bout de souffle* allows the actors to 'act out roles', Jean-Luc Godard challenges the whole basis of screen acting in one particular scene. As Michel drives from Marseilles to Paris he sings and talks to himself in the car. At one point he turns, looks directly at the camera and addresses the spectator saying: 'If you don't like the sea, if you don't like the mountains, if you don't like the big city, then get stuffed.' By allowing Michel to address the spectator Jean-Luc Godard breaks through the hermetic barrier of the cinema screen. Michel acknowledges that he is acting out a role watched by an audience and the spectator is reminded that they are watching a film.

Jean-Luc Godard's exploration of mise-en-scène, from lighting contrasts through to role-playing, creates a style which demonstrates an awareness of established cinematic conventions, and a willingness to challenge them.

## CINEMATOGRAPHY

The availability of new lightweight cameras gave Jean-Luc Godard the opportunity to shoot on location and freed him from the constraints of the studio, enabling him to approach the cinematography of *A bout de souffle* in a radical way. Cinematographer Raoul Coutard's memory of working with Jean-Luc Godard provides an insight into their approach to the film and is worth quoting at length. Writing in the 1965/66 winter edition of *Sight and Sound* he says:

> That first time, on *A bout de souffle*, he [Godard] said to me: 'No more confectionery: we're going to shoot in real light. You've been a photographer. Which stock do you prefer?' I told him I liked to work with Ilford H.P.S. Godard then had me take photographs on this stock. He compared them with others, and we made a number of tests. Finally he said: 'That's exactly what I want.'

> We got on to the Ilford works in England, and they told us that they were sorry, but their H.P.S. wasn't made for motion picture cameras, only for still photographs: we would have to give up. But Godard doesn't give up. For still camera spools, Ilford made the stock in reels of 17½ metres. The perforations weren't the same as for cinema cameras. Godard decided to stick together as many

# in a bout de souffle

17½ metre reels as he would need to make up a reel of motion picture film, and to use the camera whose sprocket holes corresponded most closely with those of the Leica – luckily, the Cameflex. The professionals were horrified.

But that wasn't the end of it. One photo-developer got particularly good results with H.P.S. stock, and that was Phenidone. With Godard and the chemist Dubois of the G.T.C. Laboratories, we ran several series of tests. We ended up by doubling the speed of the emulsion, which gave us a very good result. Godard asked the laboratory to use a Phenidone bath in developing the film. But the laboratory wouldn't play. The machines of the G.T.C. and L.T.C. laboratories handle 3,000 metres of film stock an hour, with everything going through the same developing process, and with the equipment geared to standard Kodak practice. A laboratory could not effectively take one machine out of the circuit to process film stock for M. Jean-Luc Godard, who at the very most would probably want no more than some 1,000 metres a day.

On *A bout de souffle*, however, we had a stroke of luck. Tucked away in a corner, the G.T.C. laboratories had a little supplementary machine, more or less out of service, which they used for running tests. They allowed us to borrow this little machine so that we could develop our stuck-together lengths of Ilford film in a solution of our own making, and at whatever rate we chose. There's one thing that ought to be understood: the fantastic success of *A bout de souffle*, and the turning point that this film marked in cinema history, was clearly due mainly to Jean-Luc Godard's imagination, and especially [...] to its sense of living in the moment. But it also had to do with the fact that Jean-Luc Godard stuck together these 17½ metre lengths of Ilford stock, in the teeth of everyone's advice, and miraculously obtained the use of this machine at the G.T.C. laboratories.

Jean-Luc Godard's perseverance and vanguard spirit created the remarkable results of *A bout de souffle*'s cinematography. The stylistic look of the film was unique because of the film stock and developing process chosen. However, Jean-Luc Godard's revolutionary ideas did not stop here. He and Raoul Coutard also experimented with the camera's framing and movements to create the fluid, spontaneous look of the film.

Jean-Luc Godard's framing of shots in *A bout de souffle* is more varied than in a standard Hollywood film. In the Classical Hollywood Narrative film most shots were taken within the medium long shot, mid shot and medium close-up range. Long shots were only usually used at the start of scenes to establish the location of the action. Close-ups were only employed to focus on objects or characters at particularly significant moments of the narrative. In *A bout de souffle* Jean-Luc Godard disregards these conventions to some extent. The first shot of the film starts with a close-up of the newspaper Michel is reading, denying the spectator any sense of establishing where the action is taking place. At the end of the scene where Michel and Patricia meet and walk along the Champs Elysées the camera cuts away from its position following the actors to an extreme high-angle shot, looking down as Patricia runs back towards Michel as he buys a newspaper from a news kiosk. The cut to an extreme angle is not motivated by anything of narrative importance, and thus the framing technique stands out as stylistic rather than 'functional'.

*A bout de souffle* uses a lot of close-ups, particularly on the actors' faces. For example, in the long bedroom scene the camera keeps resting on close-ups of Patricia's face. Also in this scene Patricia rolls up a poster and looks at Michel through it; the close-up effect means that Michel looks as though he is posing in a publicity still. The nature of close-ups means that they halt the narrative action, because very little action can be seen. As Jean-Luc Godard is not really interested in pursuing the action of the plot in *A bout de souffle* (see Narrative & Form) the close-ups instead serve to study the actors as they play out their fictional roles and try to work out what they want from each other. Jean-Luc Godard's style is thus suited to the overall purpose of his film.

The final key element to the look of *A bout de souffle*'s cinematography was the hand-held camera movement employed by Raoul Coutard. The new style of camera chosen by Jean-Luc Godard for the film was relatively lightweight. This was ideal for location work as it meant that the camera

# in a bout de souffle

## Godard makes the camera an active player

could be carried on the shoulder, so expensive tracks did not have to be built to move the camera. The technology gave Jean-Luc Godard the ability to be spontaneous as he could move the camera wherever and whenever he wanted.

The scene on the Champs Elysées when Patricia and Michel walk along talking is filmed in one long continuous take. Jean-Luc Godard had Raoul Coutard sit in a wheelchair holding the camera while he pushed him along to follow the actors. Another scene that consists of one long continuous take is when Michel goes to the travel agency to pick up his cheque from Tolmatchoff. Michel and Tolmatchoff start in the foyer of the agency and then walk around the corridors of the building (for no apparent reason) until Tolmatchoff is called out of the frame, leaving Michel on his own. Still the camera does not cut until Michel leaves the travel agency and the police come in. In a Classical Hollywood Narrative film the dialogue sequence between Michel and Tolmatchoff would have been filmed as a shot/reverse shot sequence. However, instead of fragmenting the scene through editing, Jean-Luc Godard's technique allows the spectator to follow the dialogue in their own way. They can choose to concentrate on Michel or Tolmatchoff, or the surroundings of the travel agency.

André Bazin admired the long takes and fluid camera movements of Italian neo-realist film-makers such as Roberto Rossellini because he believed they achieved a far 'purer' form of cinema, one which revealed the 'essential truth' of a scene through an unobtrusive camera, allowing the spectator to follow the action in their own way rather than in the way forced upon them by a film-maker using the techniques of montage or editing. However, one cannot consider Jean-Luc Godard's camera unobtrusive or passive.

Jean-Luc Godard makes the camera an active player in the construction of the film. The fact that the camera is hand-held during much of the film means that it registers the movement of the cameraman. When Patricia and Michel are being followed along the Champs Elysées and when Michel is first in the car driving from Marseilles to Paris the camera jolts around drawing attention to its active role as a mediator between the events of the diegetic world of the narrative and the spectator.

# in a bout de souffle style

continuous tracking shots

Jean-Luc Godard pushed Raoul
Coutard along the Champs Elysées
in a wheelchair to achieve long
continuous tracking shots

# in a bout de souffle

Jean-Luc Godard's approach to cinematography was completely different from that of traditional Hollywood (and French) cinema. He virtually threw away the rule book and started from scratch. Traditionally the camera and the other elements of cinematography were subservient to the narrative, their ultimate goal was not to be noticed. Jean-Luc Godard, conversely, wanted the techniques and technologies of film-making to be an integral part of his film's style. *A bout de souffle* is therefore as much a film about film-making as it is a film about a pair of lovers on the run from the police.

Jean-Luc Godard's revolutionary methods were not always understood by his crew. In a letter to Pierre Braunberger Jean-Luc Godard wrote:

> At the rushes, the entire crew, including the cameraman, thought the photography was revolting. Personally I like it. What's important is not that things should be filmed in any particular way, but simply that they should be filmed and be properly in focus. My main job is keeping the crew away from where we're shooting. (...) On Wednesday we shot a scene in full sunlight using Geva 36 film stock. They all think it stinks. My view is that it's fairly amazing. It's the first time that the maximum has been expected from film stock by making it do something it was never intended for. It's as if it was suffering from being pushed to the limit of its possibilities.
>
> *quoted in Marie, included in Susan Hayward and Ginette Vincendeau (eds)*
> *French Film Texts and Contexts, pp. 204–6*

## SOUND

Sound has often been considered the poor relation of the image in film studies. Much time has been given to the analysis of mise-en-scène and cinematography but comparatively little consideration has been given to the role of sound in the cinema. This theoretical bias denies the fundamental importance of the soundtrack in a film.

The term silent cinema is often used to refer to films made without synchronously recorded soundtracks before 1927. However, the cinema was never really silent. Music was always used to accompany the images of early films, if for no other reason than to cover over the mechanical

# in a bout de souffle    style

sound of the projection equipment. As 'sound cinema' developed after 1927 conventions for dialogue, sound effects and music developed. Diegetic sound – any dialogue, sound effects or music that can be heard by the characters within the film – added a three-dimensional depth to the image, because off-screen voices or sound effects signalled that the diegetic world existed outside the confines of the camera's frame. Non-diegetic sound – voice-overs and the musical score that the spectators hear but the characters cannot – provided the spectator with privileged information and added emotional intensity to the images on screen.

Sound effects and music have a powerful effect on a spectator's reading of a film. Certain types of music or sound will cue the spectator to read a scene as romantic or scary in a way that the image cannot achieve on its own. The sound effects or music heard in a horror film are often far more frightening than any image could be.

Throughout the Classical Hollywood Narrative cinema the traditional relationship between sound and image was a mutually supportive one. Sound and image worked to complement each other so that sound effects matched what could be seen on screen and the emotional style of a piece of music playing was appropriate. Like the other elements of film style, sound was meant to be subservient to the narrative. The conventions which governed sound kept volume, pitch, tone and timbre at a consistent level. Sharp contrasts between high- or low-pitched sound effects or quiet and loud music would potentially draw the spectator's attention to the soundtrack, making them aware of the job it was doing and distracting them from the narrative.

However, Jean-Luc Godard had other ideas about the role of sound. Rather than use sound in a way that served and followed the image he began to experiment, using sound in a stylistic way.

Throughout *A bout de souffle* Jean-Luc Godard introduces sharp contrasts in the volume of music and sound effects. For example, when Michel is driving to Paris from Marseilles he finds a gun in the car he has stolen. He points it out of the car's window at the sun and fires it, and the gunshots heard are very loud, surprising the spectator. When Michel shoots the policeman the soundtrack is relatively quiet and non-dramatic. However, as Michel is seen running across a field to escape, the musical score cuts in loudly. The soundtrack here is at odds with the two pieces of action seen and thus draws attention to the relationship between sound and image.

Jean-Luc Godard experiments even more radically with the relationship between sound and image during the scene where Michel and Patricia go into a cinema. Patricia suggests they go and see a western and when they come out of the cinema the poster shows that the film being screened was *Westbound.* However, when Michel and Patricia are in the cinema, framed in close-up kissing, the dialogue that can be heard in the auditorium is a recitation from two French poems: the first by Louis Aragon and the second by Guillaume Apollinaire. Jean-Luc Godard thus challenges the logic of diegetic sound, by including something on the diegetic soundtrack which cannot really have been heard.

Jean-Luc Godard also experiments with the conventions of sound recording when Patricia goes to interview Parvulesco at Orly airport. There is a great deal of background noise of air traffic heard. Normally this would have been present in a much quieter form, merely to provide background 'ambience' to the scene, but here Jean-Luc Godard does not tone down the sound picked up during filming, and the result is that attention is again drawn to the soundtrack. The convention of giving dialogue precedence over music and sound effects is also ignored by Jean-Luc Godard. When Patricia and Michel are talking in the bathroom during the long scene in Patricia's apartment their voices have to compete with the sound of a loud police siren from the street. In each of these examples Jean-Luc Godard is bringing the soundtrack to the fore, making the spectator aware of the role of sound within the construction of the film.

Another innovation that Jean-Luc Godard introduced in *A bout de souffle* was his approach to dialogue. Much of the dialogue spoken by Michel in the film is heavy with dialect and slang, adding to the irreverence of the film's style. To maintain the real 'essence' of Michel's dialogue, the translations for the subtitles were updated when the film was re-released in the UK in 1988. Thus the opening words of the film spoken by Michel, translated as: 'All in all, I'm a dumb bastard', in the original continuity script

# in a bout de souffle style

eclectic mix of musical styles

presented by Dudley Andrew in his book *Breathless*, are changed to: 'So, I'm a sonofabitch', in the 1988 re-release subtitles. Likewise, Michel's closing words are translated as: 'You're a real bitch', in the original version of the continuity script, and as: 'You're a real scumbag', in the updated subtitles. It's not that Michel's words in French have changed of course, but rather that the meanings associated with dialect and slang change over time. Jean-Luc Godard's use of slang for the film's dialogue challenged the conventions of spoken language in film as much as he challenged all of the other conventions of 'film language'. Everything that Jean-Luc Godard could reappraise during the making of *A bout de souffle* he did.

The soundtrack of *A bout de souffle* is also remarkable for the way it mixes a wide range of musical genres and styles. Jean-Luc Godard uses a piano jazz piece to accompany many of the scenes where Michel and Patricia make their way around Paris. The pace of this music is varied. At times it is languid, relating to the casual nature of both the characters and the narrative style. At other times it is given dramatic impetus and pace, picking up on the musical style of the Hollywood gangster B-movies which the film alludes to. Mixed in with the piece which provides the basis for the musical soundtrack are pieces of classical music. In Patricia's apartment she plays Bach, and towards the end of the film, when Patricia and Michel spend the night in Berruti's friend's apartment, Patricia puts on Mozart's Clarinet Concerto.

Added to the film's eclectic mix of musical styles are snatches of diegetic music heard from various radios. When Michel is driving from Paris to Marseilles he tunes the car radio into a number of stations and when he visits a girlfriend when he first arrives in Paris she tunes her radio to play rock and roll. During the scene in Patricia's apartment a light military tune played by a dance band is heard on the radio while Michel and Patricia wrestle under the bedclothes. Jean-Luc Godard's use of so many styles of music ran contrary to the established convention of sticking with just one style appropriate to the genre or period of the film. A host of intertextual relationships are thus set up between the film and the different genres and styles of music heard (see Contexts).

The soundtrack of *A bout de souffle* does not function merely to support

# in a bout de souffle

the image, smooth the transition between edits and provide three-dimensional depth. By exploring the potential of sound within a wider frame of reference Jean-Luc Godard allows the soundtrack to create a fresh relationship with the image, one that can be both complementary and contradictory and thus more interesting and innovative.

## EDITING

Of all of the stylistic innovations present in *A bout de souffle* it is the film's radical style of editing that has attracted the most critical attention. When quizzed by Andrew Sarris on how he hit upon the electrifying jump cuts in *A bout de souffle* Jean-Luc Godard explained:

> Unless you are very good, most first movies are too long, and you lose your rhythm and your audience over two or three hours. In fact, the first cut of *A bout de souffle* was two and a half hours and the producer said, 'You'll have to cut out one hour.' We decided to do it mathematically. We cut three seconds here, three here, three here, and later I found out I wasn't the first director to do that ... They did exactly what I did later, without knowing what they had done. Only, I said, 'Let's keep only what I like.'
>
> *from an interview published in Interview, July 1994*

The result of Jean-Luc Godard's unconventional approach to editing was that he cast aside the traditional Hollywood methods of creating temporal and spatial continuity (see Narrative & Form) and instead created his own unique style of jump cutting. An analysis of the opening few scenes of *A bout de souffle* illustrates just how radical Jean-Luc Godard's approach to editing was.

The opening shot of *A bout de souffle* is a close-up of a newspaper that Michel is reading. The image in front of the camera is of a woman in a swimsuit, and the voice of Michel is heard saying: 'So, I'm a sonofabitch. After all it's gotta be done. It has to.' By starting with a close-up Jean-Luc Godard denies the spectator the traditional establishing shot and thus the spectator is immediately 'spatially disorientated'. The camera tilts up to reveal Michel's face as he looks off-screen right. The camera then cuts to a shot of a woman. She also looks off-screen right, then left, and then she nods her head towards something off-screen right. This sequence is continued as the camera cuts back to Michel, and then back again to the woman. Here, because Jean-Luc Godard has not used an establishing shot, the spectator cannot fathom the spatial relationship between Michel and the woman, and thus the eyeline-match does not make sense. Finally, the camera cuts to show a couple walking away from a car, and the camera then pans to reveal a long shot of a harbour. The location of the action now makes sense, and the noise of a ship's horn heard during the sequence of cutting between Michel and the woman is contextualised. By using these unfamiliar editing techniques at the start of the film Jean-Luc Godard immediately disorientates the spectator and provides them with a taste of what the style of his film will be like.

Michel is shown jump-starting and stealing the car (so now the head-nodding antics make sense). He refuses to take his accomplice with him, and he drives away saying: 'Full speed ahead, Fred'. A dissolve follows, which leads into the next sequence of shots as Michel drives towards Paris. It is here that Jean-Luc Godard first introduces his technique of jump cutting. As Michel drives along the road he is singing Patricia's name. His singing is heard as continuous, yet the image cuts four times to show four different cars on the road in front of him. This disparity between soundtrack and image 'jolts' the spectator and makes them aware of the technique of editing, which under the Hollywood continuity conventions was normally effaced and made invisible. Other slight temporal jump cuts are included in this scene when Michel takes the gun from the glove compartment and plays with it.

Michel then makes the mistake of overtaking in his car and a police chase ensues. The pace of the editing mirrors the frantic nature of Michel's flight. Jean-Luc Godard also breaks the convention of the 180° rule thus disrupting the pattern of screen direction and adding to the frenetic confusion of the action. The camera shows Michel's car travelling from screen left to right, while the policemen on motorbikes are shown in pursuit going from right to left.

After the jump-leads on Michel's stolen car go he has to pull into a lay-by and it is here that he shoots the policeman. Jean-Luc Godard presents the shooting in an extremely fragmented way. There is a medium close-up of Michel's head as the policeman's voice is heard off-screen saying: 'Stop, or I'll kill you'. The camera then pans down Michel's body and cuts to a closer shot of his arm while the panning movement of the camera is continued. There is then another cut to an extreme close-up of the barrel of the gun as Michel prepares to fire. Finally, as the gunshot sounds, the camera cuts to a longer shot of the policeman as he falls backwards into the trees.

This sequence is remarkable for a number of reasons. First, the combination of close-ups and camera movement is unusual and 'uncomfortable' because the action is framed so tightly. Second, the fragmentation of the action draws attention to the way in which it has been filmed, and away from the key narrative event taking place. Finally, the shot which shows the policeman fall dead into the trees defies all spatial logic: it makes no sense for the policeman to fall here. However, it is not that Jean-Luc Godard is a bad film-maker. Aware of the conventions, he is skilfully playing with the way in which such a piece of action can be filmed.

As Michel runs away from the scene of the crime across a field the shot fades to black, making use of a conventional technique to show the passing of time. The shot fades up to reveal a change of location. Michel has arrived in Paris.

The pace of the action in the next few scenes as Michel searches for money and for Patricia is maintained by the momentum of the editing. Michel goes to Patricia's apartment first to look for her. He is shown walking across the lobby of the apartment building, and then the camera cuts to show him walking out of Patricia's bathroom, drying himself with a towel. All of the extra action which would have been shown in a Classical Hollywood Narrative film to establish where the character was and what they were doing has been cut out. Jean-Luc Godard repeats the technique in the next shot as well, which cuts from Michel in Patricia's apartment to him walking up to the bar in a café.

In the café Jean-Luc Godard once again breaks the 180° rule, as the camera films Michel first from one side of the café and then the other. Surely it is

Jean-Luc Godard's editing
technique fragments Michel's
chase with the police

# in a bout de souffle

not coincidental here that the waitress informs Michel that ham and eggs is '180 francs'.

Michel then visits a female friend. During the scene in her apartment Jean-Luc Godard again uses jump cuts to draw the spectator's attention to the form of the film's language. As Michel stands talking to the girl by her wardrobe a jump cut takes place unmotivated by any change in action and less than the standard 35 degrees necessary to change angle. After this the girl asks Michel if he has ever been a gigolo. She is now standing and he is sitting at her dressing table. Michel's response of: 'Why?' follows on immediately from her question but there has been another cut and Michel has again changed position so that he is now looking into the mirror.

Michel leaves the girl's apartment after stealing 500 francs from her. The next scene shows him at the travel agency looking for Tolmatchoff. From here he goes to find Patricia on the Champs Elysées, and the next few minutes of the film are spent in one continuous tracking shot as cinematographer Raoul Coutard follows Michel and Patricia as they walk and talk. The alternation between long takes with lots of camera movement and heavily edited sequences with lots of jump cuts persists throughout the film, varying its overall pace.

The sheer range of editing techniques present in the opening ten minutes of *A bout de souffle* is staggering. Even more so when one considers that this was Jean-Luc Godard's debut film. Jean-Luc Godard does not create and use just one style – of furious montage or the long takes and plentiful camera movement of the neo-realists. Instead he creates a mixed style, exploring the many facets of the technique of editing.

*A bout de souffle* is a film which joyously plays with all of the elements of film style, almost as though Jean-Luc Godard had discovered the magic box of film techniques and wanted to try them all out. However, Jean-Luc Godard does not do this without a purpose. Through his critical writings on *Cahiers du cinéma* he was aware of the wide range of tools available to the film auteur. As part of the New Wave Jean-Luc Godard wanted to reinvent the cinema. He did not want film style to be constrained by the demands of narrative. Rather he wanted to produce a film that unleashed the creative potential of mise-en-scène, cinematography, sound and editing.

# in a bout de souffle style

The fragmented style of *A bout de souffle*, inherent in the jump cutting, the lack of cause and effect, and the lack of 'consistency' in framing and mise-en-scène is ideally suited to the expression of the film's thematic content, which deals with a socially alienated character living in a fragmenting post-war society (see Contexts). As Arlene Croce commented in a review of the film in *Film Quarterly* in spring 1961: '*A bout de souffle*, from beginning to end, is the total expression of its own meaning. If action is all, spontaneity, improvisation, is the only possible style.'

By consciously drawing the attention of the spectator to the film techniques used, for example through the shaky hand-held camera and the contrasts in volume on the soundtrack, Jean-Luc Godard also creates a style which asks the spectator to reflect on the very process of film-making. Taking an auteur approach to Jean-Luc Godard's work, it is possible to see how his first film laid the foundations for his preoccupation with the nature of cinema, something that has lasted throughout his career.

Ultimately it is the style of *A bout de souffle* which has made the film such an enduring landmark in the history of cinema. Jean-Luc Godard's influence on subsequent generations of film-makers has been that he showed anything was possible. As Benjamin Bergery says in his article, 'Raoul Coutard: Revolutionary of the *Nouvelle Vague*', in *American Cinematographer*, March 1997:

> Even today, *A bout de souffle* endures as a masterpiece of purity and simplicity. The film trades complicated storytelling for the complex telling of straightforward stories. Every facet of the film radiates rebellion: Coutard's handheld camera, the location lighting, the pioneering use of jump cuts [...] It is a tribute to Jean-Luc Godard's vision that nearly 40 years later, the film's once-radical style appears completely contemporary.

# contexts

An analysis of the formal structure and style of *A bout de souffle* (see Narrative & Form and Style) reveals a film which radically challenged every film technique that the conventional cinema of the time took for granted. However, films do not exist in a cinematic void. They are produced within a particular historical, political, social and cultural framework which shapes their content and style, and impacts on the way in which a film is received by its contemporary audience. To further understand the impact of *A bout de souffle*, both on its contemporary society and on film culture in general it is necessary to analyse the film's relationship to the context of its production.

# historical

*A bout de souffle* was made during a period of immense social and political upheaval, both in France and throughout the western world. Europe had been devastated by the Second World War and throughout the 1950s European countries attempted to rebuild their industrial and economic base, often with the help of America. As Jill Forbes explains in her 1992 book *The Cinema in France: After the New Wave*: 'The immediate post-war period was a time when France underwent rapid and sometimes brutal modernisation, part of which was imposed by the United States as a condition of aid for reconstruction' (p. 47). 1958 was a key year in the modernisation of France as it marked the constitution of the Fifth Republic by Charles de Gaulle.

America's influence on Europe during the post-war period was not only financial. American popular culture was spread through films, music and the burgeoning medium of television, while the distribution of American consumer goods such as Coca Cola started to impact on European countries and European cultures.

One influence from American culture which had a significant impact in Europe was the rise of the 'teenager'. Youth culture, focused around rock and roll music and film stars such as James Dean and Marlon Brando, created a new identity for the young. Alienated from the 'cooperative community spirit' of the generation who had lived through the war, the young became more individualistic and focused on their own needs and desires.

# politics, morality & youth

*A bout de souffle* is not an overtly political film. (At least not in the way that Jean-Luc Godard's second feature film *Le Petit Soldat* was. *Le Petit Soldat* dealt with the French/Algerian war and was subsequently banned in France for three years). However, *A bout de souffle* provides a microcosm of France in 1959 as it explores the social politics of the time.

'Reading' the ideologies present in a film is different from reading the techniques of a film's construction. The ideological analysis of a film text requires exploration of the ways in which elements such as youth, gender and sex are represented.

The theoretical concept of representation refers to the way in which ideas about youth or gender are presented to the spectator through cinematic conventions such as costume, framing, dialogue or narrative. Analysing the representations present in films of the past is one way of uncovering the ideology and attitudes of a previous generation.

It is perhaps the lack of politics which *becomes* the politics of *A bout de souffle*. Michel appears to be apolitical and amoral. He does not discuss politics at all in the film, instead he prefers to talk about himself, money and women, for example:

```
It's like Stockholm. Everyone who comes back says:
'Swedish girls are great. I had three of them every
day. You should go!' Me, I went, and it's a lie.
First Swedish girls are ... very different from what
```

# politics, morality ...

```
they are in Paris ... and then, they are, in
general, just as ugly as Parisian girls ... No, the
only towns where the girls one meets in the street
are good-looking ... it's not Rome, not Paris, not
Rio. It's Lausanne and Geneva.
```

The film's only allusion to the politics of the day is to the parade of General de Gaulle and President Eisenhower to the Arc de Triomphe which is mentioned in the snatch of a radio broadcast heard in Patricia's hotel room. Patricia then passes by the presidential motorcade when she tries to give the detectives following her the slip. However, interestingly, the only section ordered to be cut from *A bout de souffle* by the French censors was documentary footage filmed by Jean-Luc Godard of General de Gaulle and President Eisenhower's motorcade. Although General de Gaulle's Fifth Republic encouraged the enterprising spirit of youth in its quest to modernise France and thus indirectly supported the work of the young French New Wave directors, this encouragement obviously did not stretch to a desire to appear in a film with the dubious character of Michel Poiccard.

What comes through strongly in the representation of Michel's character is his social alienation. He appears to have no real roots, no real job other than as a petty criminal, and no real goal or purpose in his life. The spectator only gathers fragmented pieces of information about Michel's background throughout the film, and the reliability of some of these bits of information is questionable. Patricia learns that Michel was married from a newspaper article, while the detectives following Michel reveal that he used to be a steward with Air France when they question Tolmatchoff. Michel really has a dual identity throughout the film. He is known as both Michel Poiccard and Laszlo Kovacs. When Patricia finds his passport in the name of Kovacs he spins her a story about it belonging to his half-brother.

Neither Michel nor Patricia display a sense of conventional morality. After discussing the death of the policeman, Patricia, wondering how the police tracked her down, says: 'That's really bad ... Informing. I think it's really bad.' Earlier in the film Michel cheerfully recounts a story about a bus driver who stole five million francs to impress a girl and had his bravado rewarded nothing left to fight for

when the girl became his look-out on robberies to maintain their lifestyle. Michel says: 'She was keeping watch. It was nice of her.'

The political and moral void which Michel and Patricia find themselves in represented the alienation and disenfranchisement felt by many young people in the late 1950s. The parents of the 1950s teenagers had been caught up in the moral crusade and purpose of the Second World War. However, the new generation often felt they had nothing left to fight for, a sentiment that was also expressed in the New Wave of literature, theatre and cinema taking place across the Channel in England.

The alienation and amorality expressed in *A bout de souffle* was shocking to some at the time of the film's release, probably because at no time does Jean-Luc Godard pass judgement on his characters. A review in *Films in Review* in March 1961 declared:

> The publicity for *A bout de souffle* says it 'has to do with two young people whose anti-social course is, perhaps, their way of facing up to the perplexing circumstances of our times.' That is a sinister declaration. It means that *A bout de souffle* upholds, and promotes, the idea that theft, murder and amoral nihilism are legitimate reactions in contemporary society. Any society which abets such propaganda is doomed.

## THE POLITICS OF SEX

The antipathy directed at the film and its characters in the above review reveals something of the unease about the social attitudes and morality captured in *A bout de souffle*. This unease also extended to the changing attitudes of young people towards sex. Prior to the Second World War sex outside marriage was considered a taboo subject throughout most of the western world. This was reinforced in Hollywood by a strict code of censorship known as the Hays Code, which throughout the 1930s and 1940s restricted the portrayal of sexual relations to the extent that even kisses were not allowed to linger for too long on the screen.

*A bout de souffle* deals with sex and promiscuity in a way that was still considered shocking in 1959. The film was banned in Australia, apparently

# politics, morality ...

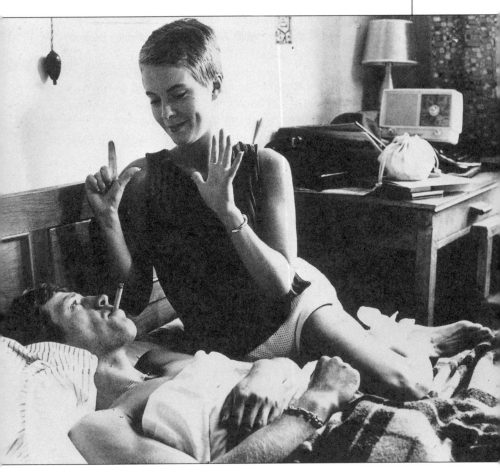

The promiscuity alluded to
in *A bout de souffle* was considered
shocking at the time of its release

because of the 'indecent nature of the subtitles when read in conjunction with the actions in the film'. While Alan Dent at the *Sunday Telegraph* wrote on 9 July 1961:

> There is one scene of 'love-in-the-afternoon' through which the British Board of Film Censors must have dozed *en masse* when it was shown to them, else they could never have allowed it to be retained.

Certainly the film is frank about sex. Michel spends most of his time trying to get Patricia to sleep with him, and Patricia's possible pregnancy means that they evidently slept together when they were on the Riviera even though they admit they only knew each other for a few days. In the scene in Patricia's apartment Michel asks: 'In New York, did you sleep with guys often?' Patricia replies: 'Not that often', and then holds up seven fingers to indicate the number of her sexual partners. When Patricia asks Michel: 'And you?', he gestures five times with his open hand, indicating that he has slept with quite a few women although he says: 'Not that many either'.

Later on in this scene Michel and Patricia finally do sleep together. The sex is represented in a fun way as Patricia and Michel wrestle under the covers, accompanied by an upbeat piece of music played by a dance band on the radio. This portrayal of sex disassociated it from the seriousness with which it was treated in mainstream cinema at the time.

The representation of sex in *A bout de souffle* is one way in which the film provides a vivid witness to its era. As Raymond Durgnat says in his retrospective of *A bout de souffle* published in *Monthly Film Bulletin* in August 1988:

> This film's specific issues (underworld loyalty, love's treachery) vividly paraphrase the alienation from old moral expectations that was swiftly spreading amongst educated youth. In particular: sexual transactions, freed at last from moral disrepute, promptly seemed void, *because* innocuous.

# representation of gender

Along with the emergence of a youth culture and the burgeoning sexual revolution, the politics of gender were also starting to change at the end of the 1950s. The Second World War brought tremendous changes in gender roles throughout Europe and America as many women had to work in industrial roles to support the war effort while men were away fighting. After the war women were often reluctant to give up their new-found independence and thus attitudes towards education and employment for women gradually started to change.

Traditionally in the cinema male stars assumed the role of protagonist, while female stars took on a supportive role. Female stars were often valued most for their looks, and thus the careers of female actresses were generally shorter than those of their male counterparts. The fact that they usually acted in a supporting role also meant that they were paid less than the male stars. Attitudes towards gender were, and are, deeply ingrained within society, and the politics of gender within the cinema extend beyond questions of the career length and pay of male and female actors. As men played the role of protagonist in the majority of film genres (with the exception of a genre such as the melodrama, where certain actresses such as Bette Davis and Joan Crawford dominated) they took on the most active role within the narrative structure of a film. Thus it was usually the male protagonist who controlled the chain of cause and effect and brought about resolution, re-equilibrium and closure. Conversely the female star was usually framed and lit in a way which objectified her, making her an object of beauty, whose role was to 'be looked at'.

The ideological representation of gender in *A bout de souffle* is complex. Michel's objectification of women throughout the film means that his actions can be read as fairly sexist, for example when he thinks about picking up two female hitchhikers on his way to Paris he says: 'Aha! A couple of dolls hitchhiking. Right, I'll stop and charge a kiss a mile. The short one's OK. She has cute thighs. Yes, but the other one! Oh no! Oh, really. Hell, they're both too ugly.' Michel 'uses' most of the women he comes into contact with, for example he refuses to take the first woman we see him with at the port in Marseilles to Paris, and then he steals money from the girl he visits in Paris. He also complains about women drivers, talks constantly about women as sex objects, and even jumps out of a taxi at one point to lift up a girl's skirt.

The views expressed by the novelist Parvulesco at the press conference attended by Patricia at Orly airport also appear to be sexist when looked at now. For example, when Patricia asks Parvulesco: 'Do you believe that woman has a role to play in modern society?', he replies, with a condescending look over the top of his glasses: 'Yes, if she is charming, if she has a striped dress and smoked sunglasses.'

As a film-maker, Jean-Luc Godard could also be accused of objectifying Jean Seberg, in the way he represents Patricia. Patricia's face often fills the screen in **close-up** and although Jean-Luc Godard did not use the lighting techniques common in the Hollywood presentation of female stars, the way in which he frames Patricia is certainly not unflattering.

Some critics are rather concerned by the representation of gender in the film. For example Tim Pulleine in a review of the film published in *Films and Filming* in August 1988 says:

> Passing over the casual elements of what might now be deemed provocatively like sexism in the movie, one comes face to face with an undertow of misogyny that is all the more powerful for seeming to be unconscious. Maybe this can be explained away by a formulaic debt to the *film noir*. But maybe not, for it now seems to be what more than anything gives the film its motivating force; and it ensures that Jean-Luc Godard's début retains, over and above its formal brilliance, a salutary capacity to disturb.

However, Patricia's role within the narrative can be seen to 'muddy' and even counteract accusations of sexism and misogyny. Although she may play the role of a coy, playful, indecisive girl when she poses pensively for the camera, denies to the detectives that she has seen Michel, and says things like: 'I don't know if I'm unhappy because I'm not free, or if I'm not free because I'm not happy', she actually has a much clearer idea of her

Patricia's character represents
the complexity of social attitudes
towards gender in the late 1950s

destiny than Michel. Patricia knows that she has to register at the Sorbonne to study in order for her parents to continue sending her money so that she can maintain her existence in Paris. She also has a clear career goal to become a writer and journalist. Patricia's journalist 'friend' Van Doude appears rather lecherous in his interest in helping her. When they meet accidentally in Montparnasse when Patricia is with Michel looking for Berutti, Van Doude 'beckons to her' and kisses her hands. However, she appears uninterested and eventually walks away from him. It would appear that she is perhaps just using him to establish her career as a journalist.

Finally, Patricia betrays Michel, not because she has an attack of morality but because she says:

> I don't want to be in love with you. That is
> why I called the police. I stayed with you
> because I wanted to be certain that I was in
> love with you ... or that I wasn't in love
> with you. And because I am mean to you ...
> it proves that I am not in love with you

Patricia is not the stereotypical femme fatale drawing the male protagonist towards his fate. She is a woman who wishes to maintain her independence and thus she takes control of the narrative at the end of the film. This is something which subverts the cinematic codes of narrative and genre, and also subverts the traditional representation of women.

Jean-Luc Godard's later films become overtly political, and in a film such as *Numéro Deux* (1975) he explores the politics of gender in a radical way. While Jean-Luc Godard's choice of a Hollywood actress to play Patricia in *A bout de souffle* might not have been very radical, and while her physical appearance as naïve and vulnerable is coded in a certain way as beautiful, Patricia is ultimately not a weak, passive character. Her decisive role within the narrative can be read as radical for the era in which the film was made, and at the same time as indicative of the ideological change of attitude towards gender present as an undercurrent at the time of the film's production.

# hollywood references

As well as the social politics evident in *A bout de souffle*, the film also provides an insight into the cultural politics of the time. *A bout de souffle* is a film full of intertextual references, making it a complex text for a spectator to read. Before the opening shot of Michel at the harbour the film opens with a title which says: 'Dedicated to Monogram Pictures.' Monogram was a small Hollywood studio making low-budget B-movies, often gangster films and film noirs, in the 1940s. Jean-Luc Godard's nod to Monogram sets out his aim to pay homage to a certain kind of Hollywood film and provides a framework for reading the film from the very start.

There are countless references to Hollywood and film-making throughout *A bout de souffle*. Michel claims that he has worked at the Italian studio Cinecittà when talking to the first girl he visits in Paris. Cinema auditoriums then provide a refuge first for Patricia, and then for Michel and Patricia when they are trying to escape from the detectives. However, the references to the cinema are evident not just on the surface of the film. Jean-Luc Godard consciously uses the codes of Hollywood genre and star to provide a cultural frame of reference for *A bout de souffle*.

Michel is obsessed with the Hollywood star Humphrey Bogart. When Michel is first shown to the audience he is rubbing his thumb across his lip, imitating an action associated with the star persona of Humphrey Bogart. Michel repeats this action throughout the film, and after he has died Patricia takes it on, rubbing her thumb across her mouth. Michel is also seen in *A bout de souffle* outside a cinema showing Humphrey Bogart's last film *The Harder they Fall* (1956). Michel stands looking at a publicity still of Humphrey Bogart from the film. The camera cuts from a close-up of the publicity still to a close-up of Michel who puffs on his cigarette and runs his thumb across his mouth, and then back again to Humphrey Bogart. The effect of the shot/reverse shot is that it sets up a mirror image, reflective of the relationship between star and spectator when a film is projected in the cinema. Michel's identification with Humphrey Bogart leads him to play out the role of Humphrey Bogart's cynical, wise-cracking star persona, so that his appearance (the hat and the cigarettes) and actions (the

Humphrey Bogart as an 'icon'

lip-rubbing and his gangster activities) create a direct relationship between
*A bout de souffle* and its predecessor Hollywood films. Even Michel's death,
as he staggers slowly down a Parisian street and then dies closing his eyes
with his own hand, is Jean-Luc Godard re-playing the death of Roy Earle
(played by Humphrey Bogart) in *High Sierra* (1941).

## GENRE

Jean-Luc Godard's use of Humphrey Bogart as an 'icon' within the film
works well because Humphrey Bogart was part of the established
iconography of the Hollywood gangster/thriller/film noir genres.
Hollywood cinema used genres to 'label' and differentiate films, for
example as westerns or musicals. Film genres are based around patterns of
repetition and variation. These patterns become familiar to spectators,
allowing them to predict a film's progress, and gain pleasure from the
expected outcome. However, each film also offers a variation on the
pattern, allowing it to be differentiated as unique. André Bazin wrote two
essays on the western genre in the 1950s and thus his colleagues at
*Cahiers du cinéma*, Jean-Luc Godard included, were familiar with the way
iconography, narrative structure and themes operated as part of the
conventions of a genre.

Jean-Luc Godard's familiarity with the narrative structure, iconography
and themes of the gangster/film noir genres is evident throughout *A bout
de souffle*. The urban Paris streets, the cars, the guns and Michel's trilby hat
mean that the film's iconography resonates with generic references.
Likewise the film's narrative and thematic structure revolve around
Michel's underworld criminal activities and his pursuit by the detectives:
the symbolic representatives of 'the law'.

However, Jean-Luc Godard has not created a straightforward genre piece.
Although he decided to remain within generic conventions by having
Michel's criminal transgressions punished by death at the end of the film,
he goes against the generic conventions of the 1950s by creating an
antihero with no redeeming features. In film noirs the protagonist is
usually lured to his death because of a fatal flaw in his character (often
that he cannot resist women, money or both). In the gangster movie the

hero normally recognises the error of his ways and thus accepts his death as reasonable justice. However, because Michel appears to be just living out the role of a movie gangster and there is no justification offered for his actions he remains an antihero until the end, making it hard for the spectator to feel emotion at his death. As Rebecca M. Pauly says in her 1993 book *The Transparent Illusion: Image and Ideology in French Text and Film* (p. 392):

> Godard constantly undermines the heroism and heroics of his simulated gangster, trivializing his moves and motives. Belmondo's narcissistic character (...) is a distorted parodic pathetic reflection of Bogie, reduced to an echo (...) But this is not Al Capone; it is rather an antihero of the post Beat generation modernists, alienated, adrift, gratuitous.

Similarly, the way in which Jean-Luc Godard brings style to the fore of the film through techniques such as the jump cut (see Style) and the way in which the characters frequently abandon the thread of the genre plot to contemplate love, sex and culture (see Narrative & Form) means that genre is denied its dominant traditional role as a structuring device.

Jean-Luc Godard's use of Hollywood generic references operates more widely as part of his project to 'take everything from cinema's history and then do it differently'. Along with the film's experimental techniques such as jump cuts and the use of a hand-held camera, the self-conscious reference to a Hollywood star and Hollywood genres means that *A bout de souffle* is a film 'about the cinema' much more than a film about Michel Poiccard's exploits.

## REFLECTING ON THE CINEMA

The film's self-reflexive theme is encapsulated in the many mirrors seen in the mise-en-scène. When Michel visits a female friend in Paris near the beginning of the film he sits at her dressing table. When the girl asks him if he has ever been a gigolo he is caught in a double-reflection. He is watching his own reflection in a small mirror as he makes a series of faces, and this is then framed within his reflection in the dressing-table mirror. Later on, in Patricia's hotel room, both Michel and Patricia make the same

holds a mirror up to Hollywood film-making

faces while looking in the bathroom mirror. Patricia has also been seen earlier, on her way back to the hotel, looking at the reflection of her body in a shop window. The mirror reflections in the film's mise-en-scène serve as a thematic comment on Jean-Luc Godard's mirroring of Hollywood techniques, genre and star. Jean-Luc Godard holds a mirror up to Hollywood film-making, and then has great fun playing with the reflection he creates.

The number of generic and cinematic references in *A bout de souffle* also means that the film can be read by a spectator on a number of different levels, depending on a spectator's prior knowledge and understanding. A spectator with an understanding of film history and culture is rewarded by their recognition of the significance of jump cuts, the references to Humphrey Bogart and the pastiche of *High Sierra* at the film's end. The inclusion of textual references to other films and film-makers, which New Wave film-makers like Jean-Luc Godard pioneered, has been carried on in the work of many modern film-makers such as Quentin Tarantino and Martin Scorsese. Brian de Palma, for instance, reconstructed the 'pram on the Odessa Steps sequence' from *Battleship Potemkin* (1925) in his 1987 film *The Untouchables*. As cinema audiences have reached a level of 'maturity' along with the medium of film, intertextual cinematic references are possible, adding depth to the way in which a film can be read.

## CULTURAL POLITICS

The references to American Hollywood culture in *A bout de souffle* are not just cinematically self-indulgent. The presence of American culture within a French film can also be read within the context of the growth of American cultural imperialism in post-war Europe. France, like most European countries after the war, was going through a period of regeneration and modernisation largely financed by the aid of the Americans. American culture was prevalent in Europe through the dominance of Hollywood, popular music and modern consumer items. The conflict between recognition of American culture and the need to preserve French culture is played out under the surface of *A bout de souffle*, and thus can be read as a subtext of the film. As Steve Smith says in his essay 'Godard and Film Noir: A Reading of *A bout de souffle*':

Despite the odds being stacked against him, Michel's obsession with American culture (or American film culture as for him they are effectively one) is what engenders and sustains the film's narrative through his desire for its principal cinematic icons: cars and women and a lifestyle to match. The film's opening scene, in which he steals the American serviceman's Oldsmobile (the first of several American cars he drives in the film) and pistol, thus serve to presage his subsequent attempt to 'steal' Patricia from the American Herald and Tribune journalist.

*from Russell King (ed.), Nottingham French Studies: French Cinema, spring 1993, p. 67*

However, as Dennis Turner points out in his essay '*Breathless*: Mirror Stage of the Nouvelle Vague', Michel's emulation of American culture is not without tension:

A bout de souffle oscillates between a belief in the inherent superiority of 'things American' – Michel Poiccard steals T-Birds and Cadillacs, courts an American girl, dresses like a Warner Brothers gangster – and the recognition that a French hero cannot attain the mythical status of the American – the cars get him in trouble with the police, the girl betrays him.

*published in Substance, 1983, vol. 12, no. 4*

# high & low cultural codes

The analysis of American popular culture in the form of Hollywood cinema was central to the work on genre and authorship carried out by the *Cahiers du cinéma* writers during the 1950s, and therefore it is no surprise that references to a Hollywood genre and star make their way into Jean-Luc Godard's first feature film. However, the textual references in *A bout de souffle* extend beyond Hollywood to a wider cultural framework. References to 'high', 'serious' artists such as Edgar Allan Poe, William Faulkner, Mozart, Bach and Renoir sit alongside those to *The Harder they Fall*, Humphrey Bogart and the western *Westbound*. As Andrew Sarris wrote in his article 'Waiting for Godard' in *Film Culture*, summer 1964:

# high & low cultural codes

tensions between realism and romanticism

> Disguised at various times as a Saganesque soap bubble and the last of the American gangster movies, *A bout de souffle* represents Jean-Luc Godard's critical vision of the cinema as a mixed form. He blithely superimposes a poem by Apollinaire on the soundtrack of what is supposed to be a Hollywood western (*Westbound*) the lovers are watching. Nor is there any strain of self-consciousness when Belmondo imitates Bogart and Seberg 'poses' for Auguste Renoir. The interplay of masks, gestures, grimaces and collages make *A bout de souffle* a film defined by unusual tensions between realism and romanticism. The director's style is personal and original, but better still, it seems to exclude the conventional middle-brow distinctions between Art and Kitsch.

The mixing of cultural codes from 'high' and 'low' art in *A bout de souffle* was part of the wider reappraisal of cultural politics and the established hierarchy of art which was central to the agenda of journals like *Cahiers du cinéma* in the 1950s.

# influences

Jean-Luc Godard and *A bout de souffle* have both proved to be extremely influential on the subsequent development of the cinema. As a 'film scholar' Jean-Luc Godard's tremendous knowledge of and passion for the cinema fed through into his films, and directors with the same passion such as Quentin Tarantino and Martin Scorsese can be seen as his direct descendants. Likewise, the energy of the stylistic innovations Jean-Luc Godard pursued in *A bout de souffle* helped to liberate popular cinema from the need to remain slavishly within the bounds of established conventions, opening the way for directors such as Quentin Tarantino and Martin Scorsese to follow as cinematic innovators.

*A bout de souffle* cannot claim to be the first film to have experimented with film form but what it, and the other New Wave films did, was to experiment and to remain popular with mainstream audiences. *A bout de souffle* achieved the rare feat of commercial and critical success on its release in France and it even managed to gain a release in the US.

# influences

The comment in American industry reviewer *Variety* on 27 January 1960 is revealing: 'With the Jean Seberg name, plus the action, this could be a playoff possibility worth dubbing. But it looms more of an arty house bet.' Very few 'foreign language' films ever make it on to the American market. The fact that *A bout de souffle* did was only due to its resounding success in France. However, its breakthrough into the American market also revealed something about the way the film industry as a whole was changing in the late 1950s and early 1960s.

The breakdown of the studio oligopolies in the 1950s due to US government anti-trust legislation and the gradual rise of the new medium of television meant that film producers could no longer rely on a regular family audience watching the films they produced every week in their cinemas. Instead, cinema audiences were both declining and fragmenting. As the older generation stayed at home to watch television a new, younger cinema audience emerged, and it is clear how a film like *A bout de souffle* would have appealed primarily to this audience.

Jean-Luc Godard's approach to the making of *A bout de souffle* was an interesting lesson for the established film industry. As audiences declined and changed, the film industry needed to be able to make films cheaply and in an innovative style that would attract a younger audience, and this is precisely what Jean-Luc Godard achieved.

Jean-Luc Godard and his New Wave compatriots (both in France and other countries like the UK) were setting themselves up as the first real 'independent film-makers'. Prior to the Second World War film-making was divided between the Hollywood studios in America, established studios in Europe and art cinema. Art cinema consisted of film-makers working entirely outside the mainstream, for example the surrealists in France in the 1920s and 1930s. Art films were distributed and exhibited completely separately from mainstream narrative films and were usually seen in specialist art-house cinemas. Vertical integration and the financial power of the Hollywood studios in striking deals throughout Europe meant that mainstream cinemas only showed the films made by the main studios. This made it virtually impossible for film-makers to work independently of the studios prior to the 1950s because they would not be able to get their films shown.

changed the structure of the film industry

However, the need for studios to sell off their cinemas as a result of the 1950s anti-trust legislation and the downturn in film audiences caused the film industry suddenly to open up to young film-makers.

One could say that Jean-Luc Godard was extremely fortunate to be in the right place at the right time. However, being there, he exploited the opportunities offered to him and he was able to pursue innovations in film style and form outside the confines of a studio system. *A bout de souffle*'s success grew out of its reputation rather than out of an international marketing campaign, and it was shown in mainstream cinemas in France despite its small production budget and experimental style.

The success of films like *A bout de souffle* changed the structure of the film industry and opened the door for film-makers such as Martin Scorsese and Francis Ford Coppola who wanted to work independently and still gain distribution to mainstream cinemas. The modern film industry is now organised around a relationship between mainstream, independent and art cinema. Mainstream cinema produces formulaic blockbusters with stars, action and special effects for a mass international audience. These films are heavily marketed over a long period of time in order to make sure (as sure as you can be in the film industry) that the studio investment in the film's massive budget is returned at the box office. Art cinema still produces individual films based around personal expression which are marketed to a niche audience and shown in arthouse cinemas in big regional centres. Independent cinema sits in the middle of the two. It is notoriously difficult to define, but is usually based around independent finance and so has smaller budgets. Independent cinema also tends to deal with less 'mainstream themes' and gives film-makers more freedom in deciding on the style of their films.

Most mainstream studios have smaller 'independent' production companies under their wing producing films like *Pulp Fiction* (1994) and *The Full Monty* (1997). Most of the innovation and diversity in film-making now comes from the independent sector because it has the freedom to experiment a little.

Jean-Luc Godard is a director who likes to provoke a reaction, and *A bout de souffle* has certainly done that during the past forty years. Critics at the

# influences

time either loved it or loathed it. Hollis Alpert wrote in the *Saturday Review* on 11 March 1961: 'Godard ... has found critical safety in mixing up the real and the unreal, and by eliminating meaning. He has set a clever trap: if nothing is said, what is there to attack? So he has made an intriguing film, but let's face it, not really a good one.' While Roger Angell commented in *The New Yorker* on 11 February 1961: 'Its virtues are so numerous and so manifest that I am confident not only that it will survive the small burden of my superlatives but that it will be revisited almost instantly by many of its viewers.'

Whatever its virtues *A bout de souffle* has survived as one of the indelible films of its era. It continues to provoke controversial opinions. When *A bout de souffle* was released on video in the UK in 1993 Richard Boston commented: 'It is all manner with no matter. This is art in a state of advanced decay' (*The Guardian,* 26 August 1993). Whereas, when the film had been re-released at the cinema in the UK in 1988 George Perry claimed:

> Often the pace-setting films are the ones in which the cliches are invented. Looking at them anew years later can prove disappointing, the freshness having been squeezed out by subsequent imitations. A pleasure, then, to report that Jean-Luc Godard's *A bout de souffle* ... is as exciting as ever.
>
> *The Sunday Times, 24 July 1988*

Whatever the views of the critics, *A bout de souffle* is part of the canon of distinguished, influential films from cinema's history. It is a regular feature on film studies courses and has been commented on and analysed in numerous academic works, many of which have been quoted from in this reading. *A bout de souffle* provides a focal point for many aspects of analysis, from the study of film techniques and film production to a consideration of the social and cultural representations found in the film.

*A bout de souffle* is a remarkable film which speaks about the cinema with exuberance, energy, vitality and audacity. The current web sites dedicated to *A bout de souffle* are testament to the fact that it is not just a film from the dusty archives of cinematic history. It still excites people when they see it for the first time.

# bibliography

## general film

Altman, Rick, *Film Genre*,
BFI, 1999
Detailed exploration of film genres

Bordwell, David, *Narration in the Fiction Film*, Routledge, 1985
A detailed study of narrative theory and structures

– – –, Staiger, Janet & Thompson, Kristin, *The Classical Hollywood Cinema: Film Style & Mode of Production to 1960*, Routledge, 1985; pbk 1995
An authoritative study of cinema as institution, it covers film style and production

– – – & Thompson, Kristin, *Film Art*, McGraw-Hill, 4th edn, 1993
An introduction to film aesthetics for the non-specialist

Branson, Gill & Stafford, Roy, *The Media Studies Handbook*, Routledge, 1996

Buckland, Warren, *Teach Yourself Film Studies*, Hodder & Stoughton, 1998
Very accessible, it gives an overview of key areas in film studies

Cook, Pam (ed.), *The Cinema Book*, BFI, 1994

Corrigan, Tim, *A Short Guide To Writing About Film*, HarperCollins, 1994
What it says: a practical guide for students

Dyer, Richard, *Stars*, BFI, 1979; pbk Indiana University Press, 1998
A good introduction to the star system

Easthope, Antony, *Classical Film Theory*, Longman, 1993
A clear overview of recent writing about film theory

Hayward, Susan, *Key Concepts in Cinema Studies*, Routledge, 1996

Hill, John & Gibson, Pamela Church (eds), *The Oxford Guide to Film Studies*, Oxford University Press, 1998
Wide-ranging standard guide

Lapsley, Robert & Westlake, Michael, *Film Theory: An Introduction*, Manchester University Press, 1994

Maltby, Richard & Craven, Ian, *Hollywood Cinema*, Blackwell, 1995
A comprehensive work on the Hollywood industry and its products

Mulvey, Laura, 'Visual Pleasure and Narrative Cinema' (1974), in *Visual and Other Pleasures*, Indiana University Press, Bloomington, 1989
The classic analysis of 'the look' and 'the male gaze' in Hollywood cinema. Also available in numerous other edited collections

Nelmes, Jill (ed.), *Introduction to Film Studies*, Routledge, 1996
Deals with several national cinemas and key concepts in film study

Nowell-Smith, Geoffrey (ed.), *The Oxford History of World Cinema*, Oxford University Press, 1996
Hugely detailed and wide-ranging with many features on 'stars'

A BOUT DE SOUFFLE

# a bout de souffle

Thomson, David, *A Biographical Dictionary of the Cinema*, Secker & Warburg, 1975
  Unashamedly driven by personal taste, but often stimulating

Truffaut, François, *Hitchcock*, Simon & Schuster, 1966, rev. edn. Touchstone, 1985
  Landmark extended interview

Turner, Graeme, *Film as Social Practice*, 2nd edn, Routledge, 1993
  Chapter four, 'Film Narrative', discusses structuralist theories of narrative

Wollen, Peter, *Signs and Meaning in the Cinema*, Viking 1972
  An important study in semiology

Readers should also explore the many relevant websites and journals. *Film Education* and *Sight and Sound* are standard reading.

Valuable websites include:

The Internet Movie Database at http://uk.imdb.com

Screensite at http://www.tcf.ua.edu/screensite/contents.html

The Media and Communications Site at the University of Aberystwyth at http://www.aber.ac.uk/~dgc/welcome.html

There are obviously many other university and studio websites which are worth exploring in relation to film studies.

# a bout de souffle

'A bout de souffle', *Variety*, 27 January 1960

'Breathless', *Films in Review*, vol. 12, no. 3, March 1961

'Personality of the Month', *Films and Filming*, vol. 7, no. 1, October 1960

Alpert, Hollis, article in *The Saturday Review*, 11 March 1961

Andrew, Dudley, *Breathless*, Rutgers, US, 1987

Angell, Roger, article in *The New Yorker*, 11 February 1961

Astruc, Alexandre, 'The birth of a new avant-garde: La Caméra-stylo', in Peter Graham (ed.) *The New Wave: Critical Landmarks*, Secker and Warburg/BFI, London, 1968

Bergery, Benjamin, 'Raoul Coutard: Revolutionary of the Nouvelle Vague', in *American Cinematographer*, vol. 78, no. 3, March 1997

Boston, Richard, 'One more wave goodbye', in *The Guardian*, 26 August 1993

Contempt.productions, http://contempt.net

Coutard, Raoul, 'Light of Day', *Sight and Sound*, vol. 35, no. 1, winter 1965/66

Croce, Arlene, article in *Film Quarterly*, spring 1961

Dent, Alan, article in *The Sunday Telegraph*, 9 July 1961

Dixon, Wheeler Winston, *The Films of Jean-Luc Godard*, State University of New York, 1997

Offers an overview of Jean-Luc Godard's career. The first chapter provides background information on the production of *A bout de souffle*

**Dudley, Andrew, *Breathless,*** Rutgers, US, 1987
The book contains a translation of the original continuity script for *A bout de souffle* as well as a selection of interviews, reviews and commentaries

**Durgnat, Raymond, 'Retrospective: *A bout de souffle*', in *Monthly Film Bulletin*,** vol. 55, no. 655, August 1988

**Forbes, Jill, *The Cinema in France after the New Wave*,** Macmillan, London, 1992

**French, Philip, article in *The Observer*,** 24 July 1988

**Gilliatt, Penelope, article in *The Observer*,** 9 July 1961

**Godard, Jean-Luc, 'But "Wave" Adds Brightness', *Films and Filming*,** vol. 7, no. 12, September 1961

**Lesage, Julia, *Jean-Luc Godard: A Guide to References and Resources*,** G.K. Hall, Boston, 1979
Provides an overview of Jean-Luc Godard's career, including credits for all of his films up to 1979. Also lists references to writings on Jean-Luc Godard and *A bout de souffle* up to 1979

**Marie, Michel, '"It really makes you sick!": Jean-Luc Godard's *A bout de souffle*,** in Susan Hayward and Ginette Vincendeau (eds), *French Film: Texts and Contexts*, Routledge, London, 1990

**Milne, Tom, (ed.), *Godard on Godard*,** Third Edition, Da Capo, New York, 1986
A collection of Jean-Luc Godard's writing and interviews, providing an insight into his thoughts on the cinema

**Pauly, Rebecca M., *The Transparent Illusion: Image and Ideology in French Text and Film*,** Peter Lang Publishing Inc., New York, 1993

**Perry, George, article in *The Sunday Times*,** 24 July 1988

**Pulleine, Tim, article in *Films and Filming*,** no. 407, August 1988

**Pulleine, Tim, article in *The Guardian*,** 21 July 1988

**Quigly, Isabel, article in *The Guardian*,** 8 July 1961

**Sarris, Andrew, 'Jean-Luc Godard Now', *Interview*,** vol. 24, no. 7, July 1994

**– – – 'Waiting for Godard', *Film Culture*,** no. 33, summer 1964

**Smith, Steve, 'Godard and Film Noir: A Reading of *A bout de souffle*',** in Russell King (ed.), *Nottingham French Studies: French Cinema*, vol. 32, no. 1, University of Nottingham, spring 1993

**Stone, Oliver, 'Riding the Crest of Chaos', in *Village Voice*,** 11 May 1972

**Temple, Michael, 'Jean-Luc Godard', in *Sight and Sound*,** vol. 8, no. 1, January 1998

**Turner, Dennis, 'Breathless: Mirror Stage of the Nouvelle Vague', *Substance*,** vol. 12, no. 4, University of Wisconsin, 1983

# cinematic terms

**180° rule** an editing technique which maintains spatial continuity and screen direction. If the camera stays on the same side of an imaginary line drawn between the actors throughout a scene then the actors will all remain consistently on one side of the image. However, if the line is crossed then an actor that was on the left of the screen will suddenly jump to the right-hand side of the screen, potentially disorientating the spectator

**35° rule** an editing technique. An edit needs to change the angle of the image by more than 35° for it to look like a 'proper' cut which has been motivated by the need to change position. An edit of less than 35° looks like a jump cut

**anti-trust legislation** brought against the Hollywood studios by the US government in the 1950s in order to break the monopoly of film-making by the studios

**art cinema** a form of cinema, separate from the mainstream, in which film-makers experiment more freely with film style. Art films are usually screened in separate arthouse cinemas

**auteur** a term describing a film-maker who is considered as an artist or the author of his or her films

**B-movies** films made cheaply by Hollywood studios to support the main feature films showing at the cinema

***Cahiers du cinéma*** a French film journal that has published debates on film theory from the 1950s to the present

**cause and effect** a technique used in Classical Hollywood Narrative films which means that every scene is linked and motivated. Nothing is included in the narrative that is not relevant, for example if a close-up of a teacup is shown then it means there is something wrong with the teacup, e.g. it is poisoned. At the end of each scene cues are given for the next, e.g. a character might say they need to investigate something and the next scene would show them in a library. What would not be shown would be their journey to the library

**cinematography** a term which describes everything related to the camera in filming: film stock, film speed, framing (i.e. the distance, level, height and angle of the camera) and camera movement

**Classical Hollywood Narrative** the system of narrative used in Hollywood films made between the 1930s and the 1950s. The Classical Hollywood Narrative system was made up of a number of narrative conventions that made films easy to follow for a mass audience

**close-up** denoting a short distance between the camera and subject/object filmed: a close-up of a person would show just one feature e.g. a face or hands

**closure** a Classical Hollywood Narrative term which describes how all the loose ends of a plot are tied up so that the narrative can be brought to a close

**continuity editing** the system of editing used in Classical Hollywood Narrative films. Continuity editing consists of a number of techniques which maintain spatial and temporal continuity even when a narrative moves between lots of locations or cuts out big chunks of time. Continuity editing

# cinematic terms

techniques are usually motivated so that they are not noticed or disruptive. This enables the spectator to concentrate on the narrative

**cultural imperialism** the domination of an indigenous culture (e.g. French culture) by the culture of another country (e.g. the US)

**cut** an edit which simply splices two shots together

**diegetic world** the fictional world in which the characters of a narrative live

**dissolve** an edit whereby one image dissolves or mixes into the next

**distribution** the process by which films are booked into cinemas. The term also describes the way films are advertised and marketed to audiences

**enunciation** the process of narrating a story. Enunciation describes *how* a story is told

**enunciator** the narrator of a story. Often in the cinema the narrator or enunciator is not made obvious, i.e. there is not a voice-over from someone who appears to be telling the story. In a situation such as this the enunciator can be considered as the film-maker

**equilibrium/disruption/re-equilibrium** describes the pattern of storytelling in Classical Hollywood Narrative films. An equilibrium (i.e. a balance) exists at the start of a narrative, a disruption occurs, and the work of the narrative is to get to the point of re-equilibrium so that harmony can be re-established within the narrative world

**establishing shot** a continuity editing technique which requires each scene of a film to start with a long shot showing the location of the action and the relative positions of characters

**exhibition** the screening of films in cinemas, on video or on television

**eyeline-match** a continuity editing technique. An eyeline-match occurs when a close-up of an actor's face is followed with a shot of another person or object. Even though the subject/ object are not physically in the frame together the spectator makes a mental link and accepts that the actor in the first shot is looking at the person or object in the second shot. This creates a three-dimensional space for the film's action from two-dimensional images

**fade** an edit whereby the image either fades up from black or fades down to black. Normally signals the end of a scene

**femme fatale** a term used to describe the female character in a film noir. Typically the femme fatale is a seductress who leads a male protagonist to commit a crime

**film noir** a term given by French critics to a genre of Hollywood films made between the 1940s and the 1950s. Film noirs were usually set in an urban criminal underworld. The visual style of film noirs was dark and shadowy. Critics believe film noirs reflected a sense of social disaffection related to the effects of the Second World War

**French New Wave** a term that describes the work of a group of young film-makers working in France from the late 1950s to the early 1960s. The French New Wave film-makers rejected the traditional style of film-making in France and started to create their own individual styles

# cinematic terms

genre  a way of classifying a type of film, for example as a western, a musical or a horror film. Each genre can be identified by visual, aural, narrative and thematic characteristics

iconography  a term describing the visual motifs/objects associated with particular genres of film. For instance, the iconography of the gangster film consists of guns, cars, smart suits and cities, while the iconography of the western consists of horses, dusty streets and cowboys

ideology  the ideas, beliefs and norms of behaviour held by a society at a particular moment in time

intertextual  the referencing of other artistic or cultural texts such as plays, novels, films, music or paintings within a text

iris  an edit, used mainly in silent films. A circle on screen closes around the image until all is black, replicating the closing down of the iris on the camera lens

Italian neo-realist  a movement of film-makers working in Italy in the late 1940s. The style of their films was commented on, particularly by André Bazin, for creating a new style of realism through location filming, the use of non-actors, long takes and lots of camera movement

jump cut  an edit which appears to 'jump', either because time jumps forward on the image track but not on the soundtrack, or because the camera has not been moved by more than a 35° angle

long shot  denoting a long distance between the camera and subject/object filmed: a long shot of a person would show the whole of their body and their background and location

match-on-action  a continuity editing technique. A match-on-action is when an edit takes place in the middle of an action. For example, shot one might show a person sitting down while shot two shows them standing up. The cut occurs during the movement from sitting to standing. This ensures that the edit goes unnoticed because the spectator is distracted by the act of movement itself

medium close-up  denoting a short to medium distance between the camera and subject/object filmed: a medium close-up of a person would show their body from the chest upwards

medium long shot  denoting a medium to long distance between the camera and subject/object filmed: a medium long shot of a person would show the whole of their body

mid shot  denoting a medium distance between the camera and subject/object filmed: a mid shot of a person would show their body from the waist up

mise-en-scène  from the French term meaning 'put in to the scene'. Describes everything in the image which has been placed in front of the camera for filming: set design, location, costume, make-up, props, actors, acting style and lighting effects

overlapping sound  a continuity editing technique which links scenes together. As one scene ends and the next begins any music playing in the first scene is carried over to the start of the next scene

# cinematic terms

pan   a camera movement, where the camera head moves horizontally from side to side

*politique des auteurs*   published in *Cahiers du cinéma*, the *politique des auteurs* called for the rejection of the traditional French 'cinema of quality' in favour of a cinema which would allow individual film-makers to express themselves as artists

protagonist   the main character within a narrative, usually 'the hero'. Everything in a Classical Hollywood Narrative film revolves around the protagonist

representation   a term that describes the cinematic presentation of ideological constructs such as gender, race, age, class and sexuality

shot/reverse shot   a continuity editing technique used for dialogue scenes. First both of the actors engaged in a conversation are shown in a two-shot, then the camera cuts in to mid shots and close-ups of one actor and then the other, usually from a position 'over the shoulder' of the other actor. This pattern allows long dialogue scenes to be broken down, so that the spectator sees the significant facial expressions and reactions of the actors as they speak

stars   term describing the leading actors and actresses in Hollywood films

star system   describes the way a star's image is promoted in order to sell a film

studios   the studios, e.g. Warner Brothers, MGM, and Paramount, controlled the whole process of film production from the 1920s to the 1950s

studio system   describes the way in which the studios organised the production, distribution and exhibition of their films

tracking shot   a camera movement where the camera is moved forwards, backwards or to the side

vertical integration   a term which describes how the studios had control of every stage of film production, distribution and exhibition between the 1920s and the 1950s. The studios financed films, produced them in their own studios, publicised them and then screened them in the cinemas they owned. Vertical integration meant that the studios could monopolise film production

wipe   an edit whereby one image is wiped horizontally or vertically across another to replace it

A BOUT DE SOUFFLE

# credits

## production companies
Société Nouvelle de Cinematographie,
Productions Georges de Beauregard, Impéria Films

## director
Jean-Luc Godard

## producer
Georges de Beauregard

## screenplay
Jean-Luc Godard

## photography
Raoul Coutard

## editor
Cécile Decugis

## music
Martial Solal

## sound
Jacques Maumont

## assistant director
Pierre Rissient

## original idea
François Truffaut

## camera operator
Claude Beausoleil

## assistant editor
Lila Herman

## technical consultant
Claude Chabrol

## distributors
France - Impéria Films
UK - B.L.C., British Lion
US - Contemporary/McGraw-Hill

## length
90 minutes, 8104ft

## shooting schedule
August 17 - September 15 1959

## release
French release: March 1960
US release (as *Breathless*): February 1961
UK release: (as *Breathless*) July 1961

## cast
Michel Poiccard, aka Laszlo Kovacs - Jean-Paul Belmondo
Patricia Franchini - Jean Seberg
Inspector Vital - Daniel Boulanger
Antonio Berruti - Henri-Jacques Huet
Liliane - Liliane David
Carl Zombach - Roger Hanin
Van Doude - Van Doude
Second inspector - Michel Favre
Parvulesco - Jean-Pierre Melville
Used car dealer - Claude Mansard
Informer - Jean-Luc Godard
Journalist - Jean-Louis Richard
Drunk - Jean Domarchi
Tolmatchoff - Richard Balducci
Journalist at Orly - André S. Labarthe
Journalist at Orly - François Moreuil

# Other titles in the series

**Other titles available in the York Film Notes series:**

| Title | ISBN |
| --- | --- |
| 8½ (Otto e mezzo) | 0582 40488 6 |
| Apocalypse Now | 0582 43183 2 |
| Battleship Potemkin | 0582 40490 8 |
| Blade Runner | 0582 43198 0 |
| Casablanca | 0582 43200 6 |
| Chinatown | 0582 43199 9 |
| Citizen Kane | 0582 40493 2 |
| Das Cabinet des Dr Caligari | 0582 40494 0 |
| Double Indemnity | 0582 43196 4 |
| Dracula | 0582 43197 2 |
| Easy Rider | 0582 43195 6 |
| Fargo | 0582 43193 X |
| Fear Eats the Soul | 0582 43224 3 |
| La Haine | 0582 43194 8 |
| Lawrence of Arabia | 0582 43192 1 |
| Psycho | 0582 43191 3 |
| Pulp Fiction | 0582 40510 6 |
| Romeo and Juliet | 0582 43189 1 |
| Some Like It Hot | 0582 40503 3 |
| Stagecoach | 0582 43187 5 |
| Taxi Driver | 0582 40506 8 |
| The Full Monty | 0582 43181 6 |
| The Godfather | 0582 43188 3 |
| The Piano | 0582 43190 5 |
| The Searchers | 0582 40510 6 |
| The Terminator | 0582 43186 7 |
| The Third Man | 0582 40511 4 |
| Thelma and Louise | 0582 43184 0 |
| Unforgiven | 0582 43185 9 |

# Also from York Notes

Also available in the **York Notes** range:

## York Notes
The ultimate literature guides for GCSE students (or equivalent levels)

## York Notes Advanced
Literature guides for A-level and undergraduate students (or equivalent levels)

## York Personal Tutors
Personal tutoring on essential GCSE English and Maths topics

*Available from good bookshops.*
For full details, please visit our website at www.longman-yorknotes.com

# notes

# notes

# notes

# notes

# notes